Teachers *are* Burdened

Teachers *are* Burdened

Proven Tips to Lighten the Load and Win

Janice Scott Cover, EdD

ARCHWAY PUBLISHING

Copyright © 2020 Janice Scott Cover, EdD.

All rights reserved. No part of this book may be used or reproduced by any means, graphic, electronic, or mechanical, including photocopying, recording, taping or by any information storage retrieval system without the written permission of the author except in the case of brief quotations embodied in critical articles and reviews.

Archway Publishing books may be ordered through booksellers or by contacting:

Archway Publishing
1663 Liberty Drive
Bloomington, IN 47403
www.archwaypublishing.com
1 (888) 242-5904

Because of the dynamic nature of the Internet, any web addresses or links contained in this book may have changed since publication and may no longer be valid. The views expressed in this work are solely those of the author and do not necessarily reflect the views of the publisher, and the publisher hereby disclaims any responsibility for them.

Any people depicted in stock imagery provided by Getty Images are models, and such images are being used for illustrative purposes only. Certain stock imagery © Getty Images.

Scripture quotations are taken from the King James Version of the Bible.

ISBN: 978-1-4808-8463-2 (sc)
ISBN: 978-1-4808-8462-5 (hc)
ISBN: 978-1-4808-8464-9 (e)

Library of Congress Control Number: 2019921232

Print information available on the last page.

Archway Publishing rev. date: 01/27/2020

To all the folks who made a significant difference in my life:

Ms. Mack, Mrs. Haughton, Mrs. Maynard Henry,
my teachers who nurtured my dreams,

my dedicated staff who placed children first,

and my many supervisors and mentors who showed me how

Alexander, Gwendolyn Scott, and my dear
brother Karl, I wish you were still here.

Patrice, Marlon, and Julian, I press forward because of you.

Patrick, my soul mate, we have landed on solid ground.

Granddaughters Elise and Eva, you have been game changers.

Jean and Patsy, my sisters, what a journey!

Contents

Introduction ix
Acknowledgments xiii

1 I was Born to Teach 1
2 Look Inside 11
3 Test 27
4 Confront Your Truth 35
5 Communicate to Elevate 45
6 Practice Healthy Habits 53
7 Set Goals 63
8 Maximize Learning 69
9 Do Without 77
10 Network 85
11 Appreciate and Ignore Naysayers 93
12 Believe 101
13 Manage Details 109

14 Give 115

15 Watch the Money 123

16 Live Life with Urgency 131

Reference List 137

Introduction

TEACHERS DESERVE AN ETERNITY OF COMMENDATIONS. A teacher's dedication to the job is unmatched. All my life, I have been a student shaped by dedicated and inspiring teachers who have left an indelible mark on my life, an impact so tremendous that for approximately four decades, I have served as a teacher, working tirelessly to do for others what my teachers did for me.

Teachers are the cornerstone of society. Communities rely heavily on educators' wisdom and therefore place enormous confidence in their abilities to frame an educated, democratic, and competitive nation.

Teachers are also surrogate parents. It is not unusual to see teachers visiting sick students in the hospitals. Educators show scholars how to be compassionate human beings. Despite receiving an inadequate paycheck, teachers still manage to purchase breakfast and lunch for needy students, not to mention the funds doled out to buy clothes, shoes, and school supplies.

In the classroom, teachers are role models to students who, like me, work hard to please and to emulate school heroes who teach reading, essay writing, arithmetic, and equally as crucial, valuable life lessons. I know that pupils thrive in classes where teachers are facilitators, providing meaningful learning opportunities in a positive environment, where cooperative learning and analytical and creative thinking are the norm. When teachers are empathetic and respectful, students learn and practice similar behaviors.

Future leaders, inventors, scientists, teachers, medical and legal experts, caregivers, and a variety of service providers show up in classrooms every year relying on teachers. My heroes, teachers, impact lives and society by being knowledgeable of academic subjects while using innovative methods to bring the content to life.

Throughout my career, I learned and implemented strategies to motivate, encourage, and support students and staff alike. Through trial and error, being knocked down a few times but refusing to stay down, learning from my experiences and through the practices of others, I gleaned a wealth of wisdom and strategies that have shaped my life and career.

I began my career in a first-grade classroom located in a small rural village on the beautiful island of Jamaica, where I was born. Over several decades, I have served diverse communities in numerous instructional and administrative positions. Despite some slips and falls, I successfully navigated a path up the career ladder to have a voice at the decision-making table of the eleventh largest school district in the United States. Over the years, I proudly acquired several degrees and participated in infinite training, yet some of the most impactful and lasting tutelages emanated from daily interactions with people of all ages and backgrounds, not to mention lessons learned through trial and error occurrences.

After forty years, my journey continues with renewed drive, commitment, and determination to be a beacon of hope and resource for students and teachers, no matter their location and situation.

My village of students, teachers and mentors helped to crystallize my purpose, and I am truly grateful for the priceless lessons that I pledge to always share.

I wrote this book to teach what I have been learning and to assure my fellow educators that they too can achieve personal and professional success for themselves and students in their charge that will inevitably leave an eternal impact.

This book also serves as a teaching tool. The "Teachers' Corner" at the end of each chapter will pose questions and ideas for discussion and reflection, hopefully bringing about necessary change. Like so many teachers with whom I interact, I too grapple with some of the big ideas about how to prepare my students and myself adequately for the excitement and challenges of the twenty-first century. In this attempt, I continually evaluate my teaching approach and adjust my behaviors and beliefs to improve my life and those of the people with whom I come in contact.

I hope readers will take time to ponder and respond to the thought-provoking questions. Knowing that there is reinforced courage when two or more collaborate, I suggest gathering a group of friends and coworkers to join the debate candidly by answering the questions and completing the suggested end-of-chapter activities. Not only will a professional learning community be strengthened and isolation among and between faculty and staff reduced, but teams will also amass a wealth of fascinating ideas and strategies geared toward improving academic, social, and emotional needs of students. Below are a few sample questions and things to consider.

Teachers' Corner

1. If you had an opportunity for a professional "do-over," what would you do?

2. Describe the personal or professional impact you believe you have had in your school and community.

3. What is your teaching/learning style?

Hopefully, my personal stories throughout the book will affirm as well as invigorate your journey and challenge your beliefs about teaching and learning while driving you to further personal growth and development. Each chapter also concludes with "Digging In" activities to help in organizing, developing, and implementing winning strategies. Below are sample suggestions.

Digging In

1. Become an active participant in extracurricular activities in your work environment and the community. Join the parent-teacher organization or a civic group like the local Kiwanis Club.

2. Volunteer to be a mentor to a student at your school. Meet with your mentee regularly to discuss school progress or goal setting.

3. Volunteer to be a buddy/supporter to a new coworker or one experiencing instructional or classroom management difficulties. Meet informally to plan lessons and exchange effective student improvement strategies.

Acknowledgments

I WOULD NOT HAVE KNOWN THE VALUE OF EDUCATION had my parents, Gwendolyn Freeman Scott and Alexander Augustus Scott, not stressed the importance. My mama and daddy made unbelievable sacrifices to ensure that I received and took advantage of the schooling they never had. I will be forever grateful for their example and support. I know their job continues as my guardian angels.

There were countless teachers in my life who saw my potential even when I could not, starting with Ms. Mack, my primary school teacher who taught me to read, a skill that gave me a strong early academic start and boosted my self-confidence. Mrs. Haughton, my elementary school teacher and principal, taught me that hard work and perseverance would make the difference between succeeding and not. For years, I planned the right words to express my gratitude, and that moment came recently. I owe you an enormous debt. I will always aspire to be like Mrs. Maynard Henry, my Spanish teacher and mentor at Dunrobin High School, who saw the needs of the little country girl, missing her family and struggling to assimilate into boarding life and stresses of city living while fully immersed in high school. You saw the teacher in me. You protected me like a mother to her daughter, and I will never forget your kindness.

To my countless students at Martin Primary, Hope Bay All Age, and Tarrant High Schools in Jamaica, you taught me how to teach. My sixth graders at Buchanan Elementary School in my USA internship class, you challenged me to be a better teacher and broadened my perspective about teaching in urban settings. Amelia Ostrosky, former principal at Allamanda Elementary School in Florida, you placed the administrative bug in my ear and provided numerous opportunities for me to learn and grow. I will forever remember the freedom I had to be innovative and scholarly at Allamanda. I was new to the school system, and you, the community and parents, coworkers and students were most gracious.

To the staff at Timber Trace, Allamanda, and Pine Grove Elementary Schools, in addition to John F. Kennedy Middle School, your commitment, professionalism, and dedication softened the demands of an otherwise challenging job. I learned so much from visiting your classrooms, observing your diverse teaching styles, and interacting with students. Through ongoing collaboration, problem-solving, and development of unique programs, we successfully changed the lives of endless numbers of students and families.

To you, my countless students at Nova Southeastern University and Palm Beach State College, you helped to advance my research and presentation skills, most importantly keeping me abreast of the ever-changing social media norms and language.

Former superintendent of schools Dr. Arthur Johnson, you gave me the shock of my life when you promoted me to the position of director of elementary schools in the eleventh largest school district in the United States—and shortly after to assistant superintendent. In these roles, I drew on a wide range of experiences from previous jobs and worked with dedicated employees to improve departments' functioning, offer support to schools, and showcase talent in our school district.

1

I was Born to Teach

THERE IS AN ONGOING DISCUSSION ABOUT WHETHER teachers are born or made. Opinions vary based on observable assessments of teachers, such as whether they are caring, knowledgeable, competent, passionate, kind, flexible, hardworking, determined, and intuitive, to name just a few. There are persons within the profession who are on both sides of the argument. No doubt the debate will continue, but one thing I know without reservations: I was born to be a teacher. Picture a five-year-old child living in a rural Jamaican village whose only dream is to become a teacher and, as a result, started modeling the practices of teachers around her.

Since the early days, I have had numerous role models and in-field experts who supported my dream and helped to shape my career. I salute my teachers, starting with my preschool teacher, Ms. Mack, who got me on the right path. She was a well-respected teacher who operated the little school for several years. If you were born in that community, chances are good that Ms. Mack was your infant-school teacher.

She took my three-year-old blank slate and miraculously taught me how to read and write letters of the alphabet and count numerals using an unsophisticated black-and-white with yellow cover pre-primer book measuring approximately four by six inches and containing about thirty pages. This tiny book, made in Hong Kong, was organized into two sections. Part 1 focused on short vowel sounds, and part 2 taught long vowel sounds and included short sentences.

Quite early I learned to write my name, spell simple words, and memorize nursery rhymes and Bible verses. I listened to traditional fairy tales and Jamaican folktales and was always mesmerized by my teacher's enthusiasm when she read aloud from the few storybooks she possessed. I quickly learned to read and became a proficient reader before I left preschool. In addition to laying a strong academic foundation, Ms. Mack reinforced social skills such as kindness, respect for all, and helpfulness, reminding us to always say please and thank you—behaviors my parents taught at home.

I wanted to be like Ms. Mack. When I started teaching, I tried to teach children how to read, write, and compute at high levels, just as my basic-school teacher did. Significantly, I wanted my students to feel safe, to be risk-takers, and to thrive in an environment like the one Ms. Mack created for me.

Beginning with my preschool teacher, I learned to respect and admire the dedication and commitment of teachers. A one-room church building housed our portable school. Each morning Ms. Mack had the arduous task of carting the school supplies from her house up the hill to the church, only to repeat the steps at the end of the day. When it rained heavily, making it difficult to lug the supplies and equipment back and forth, school was held at her tiny wood-framed house, suitable for just one person.

While in school, whether we were sitting on the church benches with our short feet struggling to find balance on the floor and our infant laps serving as desks for our slates, or we were sitting on the floor in the teacher's tiny wooden house, the reverberating message conveyed and well received was that we could and would learn. The physical setting may not have been ideal compared to today's standards, but looking back, I know those humble beginnings served as an inspiration to try hard, to strive for a better life.

I was a little girl full of energy and passion who happily became a teacher's pet, helping my teacher and classmates. I assisted the children with learning letters and numbers that I had already mastered. I was also my teacher's gofer. I can still remember the sense of pride and boost to my confidence level when I lead the chanting of nursery rhymes and memorization of Bible verses. I felt like a teacher directing her classroom and modeling expected behaviors.

I always fulfilled my pretend teacher responsibilities with enthusiasm. I became a leader before I even knew the word. As I helped the teacher and other students, I developed a sense of community, a concept handed down from my parents, who always found ways to help others. I learned early that we all have something to contribute to society. Oral and written communication activities were part of our daily school routine. We sang, played games, and memorized and acted out poems. We practiced penmanship and studied big words. Importantly, my direct involvement as a student leader kept a smile on my face and my shoulders erect with pride. I thrived with Ms. Mack. I had regular affirmations of how success looked and felt. I was happy. In my young mind, I was a teacher.

At home, I used the side of our wood-framed house as a chalkboard. The shrubbery, flowers, and small plants that grew alongside the house were my unwitting students. On weekends and during summer breaks, the yard was my classroom. I had a teacher's voice and a student's voice, asking and answering the questions myself.

When I transitioned from preschool to elementary school, I met teachers who exceeded Ms. Mack's impressive instructional and personal qualities. I have fond memories of my first day of "big" school. I remember the teacher's amazement with the speed in which I completed each assigned task. It was apparent that I had some advanced academic skills, so she transferred me to a higher grade. The same situation occurred in the new class. I was promoted twice by the end of my first day. Before the first week of school ended, I was a third-grade student.

With my best interest as the priority and no external rules or bureaucracies to cripple their decision, the school had the autonomy to transfer me. Looking back, I am glad options were available for me to progress at my pace and learning abilities rather than being restricted with rules having to do with a student's age. I excelled.

Those early days in my rural community, there was no knowledge of gifted education. However, Principal Haughton, with her infinite wisdom, created a class for me and about ten other students who were also surpassing grade-level expectations. I spent the remainder of my elementary school years feeling exceptional and behaving brilliantly in this one-of-a-kind class.

My teacher preparation continued in elementary school, which, like the preschool, had an open concept: no barriers or walls between each class. The design allowed me the opportunity to observe the various teaching styles around me. I was fascinated with the different classroom management techniques. Yes, in those days, corporal punishment was practiced in schools, but not every teacher used the strap. I witnessed one-on-one redirecting of off-task behaviors and classmates being encouraged to help their peers. I saw how teachers-built rapport with students. Our teachers were masters at differentiating instruction, moving between desks to help students or check on progress. My teachers showed me the tone instructors should use. I was a silent spectator, absorbing each word and contemplating every move.

As a young child, I was an avid reader who loved literary classics and was curious about the books read in other classes. Soon I became a reading buddy, having mature book talks with teachers and older students. In addition to being swept away through books to exotic faraway places and getting a worldview on different topics, I learned through the shared reading experience that teachers are real people who find ways to connect with students.

As I matured, so did my make-believe teaching practices. During recess at my elementary school, I recruited my peers to be my students; I was the teacher, and I "kept school." Our location was under a huge tree with wide branches that provided shade from the warm Jamaican sun. I habitually rushed to the classroom underneath the tree to secure my spot before others claimed it for playground activities. I needed to prepare the space for my recess classroom. I modeled my teachers, who reported to school early to plan and organize the day's lessons.

Effective teachers know their subject matter and implement innovative strategies to motivate and educate each student. I was blossoming in all my subjects, so, like most teachers, I taught what I knew to my students. In my outdoor classroom, I mimicked the curriculum used in my regular classroom. I was exceptionally bright in English grammar and writing compositions. Therefore, my focus was on my strengths. We also told stories and composed and performed custom-made plays.

My teaching activity always competed with recess time, so I had the ongoing task of recruiting students. Some came willingly. Others did not. I believe the reluctant participants showed up because the fun activities made them feel happy and as if they belonged. We sang inspirational songs and played ring games. We had track-and-field competitions. The only prize was the opportunity to participate.

Unconsciously, teaching my peers provided invaluable training on issues like student motivation and classroom management—challenges many teachers encounter. Despite my primitiveness and innocence about what works in schools, the recess activity taught me that school must be a special place and that there are certain things that teachers do daily to enhance teaching and learning. These lessons remained with me throughout my career.

I met another gem in my high school Spanish teacher, Mrs. Maynard Henry. She quickly recognized my passion for learning and aptitude for teaching. She became my mentor. On several occasions, I was her private substitute teacher. I taught Spanish to her classes while she graded papers. While I was never left alone in the classroom with my peers, I was confident with the subject matter and my abilities to present, so I knew I would have done a superb job if I had had full control of the class. I will always appreciate her vote of confidence and investment in me. The boost to my teenage self-esteem was another proof that teachers, with the appropriate strategies, can nurture enthusiasm, passion, and lifelong skills in children.

During my senior year, Mrs. Maynard Henry helped me get a teacher's helper job at a nearby preschool. I worked with the young children during my study hour and sometimes after school. Besides the incredible experience of working in a classroom environment, I got a small but significant stipend. I saved my earnings and was able to fund all expenses for my senior year and graduation activities. A thoughtful little act can make a considerable difference in a child's life.

In English literature class, I was regularly called on to analyze a puzzling poem or to share my interpretation of excerpts from Shakespearean literature. The more I explained and made inferences about the characters and events, the better I got. Children need continuous opportunities to show and practice what they know. I was also able to transfer skills and information to other subjects, create deeper understandings, and expand my knowledge across the curriculum. I can still remember my excitement to talk about and share my opinions on quotes like "pound of flesh" in *The Merchant of Venice* (Shakespeare 1991). My enthusiasm, passion for learning and opportunity to express points of view helped position me to the title of expert, which I wore with great pride. My peers came to rely on my class participation. Little did I know that years later I would become an interim literature teacher at the same school. Another outgrowth from my active class participation is my ability to speak with ease in audiences of any size.

I am proof that teachers do more than teach subjects. When teachers take a personal interest in the growth and development of students, chances are that success is inevitable. I was a little country girl with a fervent desire to be a teacher. I was relentless in pursuit of my dreams, which took me into numerous classrooms and allowed me to meet students from various upbringings.

Over the years, I was fortunate to have taught at all grade levels, from kindergarten through to the twelfth grade, as well as in post-secondary and college programs. Along the way, my ability to lead grew more apparent, so I grasped opportunities and acquired certification and training in educational leadership. My hard work and determination opened doors that were beyond my initial dreams of being a classroom teacher. The leadership phase of my career began with school level administration and then advanced to the central office, serving as director of elementary education and assistant superintendent, managing large budgets for significant programs like Exceptional Student Education (ESE) and Alternative Education, and spearheading the state's equity in education compliance requirements for my school district. I have often heard the phrase "once a teacher, always a teacher," so notwithstanding leadership positions and administrative roles, I always found ways to feed my passion for teaching. I inherently believed that I had a responsibility to help all my students' progress, and this became my philosophy throughout my teaching career.

I am a proponent of sharing ideas and best practices that were instrumental in helping me achieve beyond my wildest dreams. Hence, this book presents strategies and approaches that bolstered my journey. During my four-decade adventure, I made significant personal strides, and most of all, I managed to positively impact the lives of countless students of all ages and situations, contribute to the dialogue about urban education, and specifically master strategies about teaching and learning. I have become an invaluable resource for numerous aspiring and veteran educators. This book supports the notion that an effective teacher is the essential school factor contributing to student achievement. The book also purports that a principal is the school's primary cheerleader. To that end, strategies in the book apply to all educators as well as anyone on a path for self-improvement.

Teachers' Corner

1. Teachers in my life largely influenced and supported my career. Who or what was the deciding factor for you to become an educator?

2. List ten characteristics of effective teachers.

3. Are you an effective teacher? If so, how do you know?

4. What are your thoughts about the statement "Teachers are born, not made or trained"?

5. Write at least ten comments that you hope to hear at your retirement party.

6. Do you know any teachers who should be encouraged to choose another vocation or profession? If so, why do you think so?

7. What is teacher burnout? Describe some symptoms.

8. Given a choice, would you leave the teaching profession? If so, why?

9. How prepared were you for the job you currently hold?

10. Suppose your supervisor requested that you make a presentation at the next faculty and staff meeting, sharing ten valid student achievement strategies. Which strategies would you discuss?

Digging In

1. Find at least five trusted friends and confidants to share your professional dreams and aspirations. Develop measurable goals and create individual visions together. Establish regular meeting times to discuss progress toward the goals and to celebrate successes.

2. Develop a personal teaching philosophy. When the semester or school year ends, revisit the document and adjust as needed.

3. Routinely implement differentiated instruction with flexible learning groups to provide for the diverse learning abilities and learning styles of students.

4. Give students opportunities to teach. When they can articulate the information, you can be assured they know the material.

5. Volunteer to teach at another grade level or a subject for which you hold certification.

2

Look Inside

TEACHING IS ONE OF THE MOST SCRUTINIZED PROFESsions. Teachers tend to get caught in the middle of continual policy and administrative changes and decisions, mostly focused on areas of school reform, student assessment, and teacher evaluations. In this era of standardization and high-stakes testing, the responsibility for student performance and school success rests on the overworked shoulders of teachers. Not to mention the never-ending sizing up that is dished out by students, parents, and respective communities.

Each year teachers leave the profession citing undue stress as one contributing factor. Alarmingly, a high percentage of the departed exit during the first three years. Still, millions, like me, remain for a variety of reasons; despite many challenging moments, the benefits of making a difference are priceless.

We know teaching is complex, ensuring all students meet established standards, administering and analyzing ongoing assessments, regularly researching effective methods to improve teaching and learning plus executing innovative methods to manage overcrowded classrooms of deserving learners. It is the teacher's responsibility to adhere to federal, state, and local education mandates while providing for the developmental needs of each student. Teachers must be cheerleaders for students, calm anxieties around unpopular assessments, ensure that the appropriate subject area content is taught at the pertinent time, and deal with social and emotional issues, in addition to handle growing disquiet about increased occurrences of classroom observations and feedback from school administration.

A perceived negative feedback or comment has some teachers, including me, question their abilities to carry out certain tasks effectively, preparing students, and at the same time remaining composed and confident to teach all students. In my early years, I grew weary and sometimes lost sleep, uncertain how supervisors viewed my teaching abilities. Over time, I developed some courage. I refrained from internalizing the unfavorable remarks and started listening to what was being said, which led to thoughtful introspection, learning to let go of the things over which I had no control, accepting my own limitations regarding constantly changing curriculum and testing, and trying to control the negative effects of students' out-of-school lives on academic performance.

The process of looking within helped me to understand that despite my hard work, there would be complaints and some dissatisfied people. My main job was to develop quality lessons based on research, use test results to inform instruction, collaborate and ask for help, and continuously seek ways to maximize students' learning.

So as an educator, how do you examine your skills? Are you an objective evaluator? Do you use a research-based tool to guide you? How do you handle and respond to results from self or evaluation from others? Like it or not, one certainty in our profession is the ongoing evaluation of students and teachers. We add to the pressure by being extremely hard and less forgiving of ourselves. I test myself every day.

Speaking of being tested, one teaching assignment that had me always checking my skills and abilities was my initial teaching experience in Louisiana, where I also completed my first United States of America teaching degree. The sixth-grade class consisted of twelve students, ten boys and two girls. All of the students had been previously retained one or more times throughout their school life. Student behaviors were so atrocious that integrating with other students was prohibited. Housed in a portable building at the rear of the campus, the twelve students ate breakfast and lunch in the classroom, not in the school cafeteria with other classes.

My initial observation of the class showed an unmotivated, unruly, and severely academically deficient group of students who mimicked each other's behaviors and whose primary goal was to chase me off as they had done to three teachers before me. However, I had a surprise for them. First, giving up was never part of my disposition; second, I was eager to restart my teaching career; and more importantly, I was determined to show them an alternative path. I also knew that one of my roles as their teacher was to help them see and believe in their possibilities, to show them how to set and achieve personal and group goals, and experience success. I set out to prove success was possible. Of course, there were many days when I questioned my optimism.

Wasting no time, the students and I started the evaluation of each other, each for a different purpose. Eventually we created a guide for classroom endurance. We established a pact around respect for each other and the teacher. To begin the process for achieving academic and behavioral success, the plan required completion of all classwork and homework, staying focused during class, and being open to accepting help. We agreed that there would be no put-downs of each other, and we practiced using supportive words like "good job," "way to go," "I am proud of you," and "you did it." We created a buddy system. The buddy was a class friend who may be a tutor but sometimes a friend to help de-escalate a situation when appropriate. We pledged to support each other. Activities such as free time or playing board games served as rewards.

Each day I taught the necessary grade-level skills and simultaneously remediated missing skills using fun activities and cooperative learning strategies. In reading, one favorite activity was making story predictions based on titles and topic sentences and then collaboratively checking hypotheses. Hands-on math lessons were based on real-world situations like physically measuring, weighing, and using play money to buy and sell goods.

As time progressed, I realized the students liked academic challenges and showed eagerness to learn. Class participation increased. I modeled how to find and use information in textbooks and encyclopedias (there was no classroom internet back then). Research also included conducting interviews with family and friends. I showed them the purposes of and how to use a dictionary. We did extended activities around topics and skills such as performing science experiments. As trust and behaviors improved, we ventured out of the classroom to explore art, beauty, and patterns in nature. We created songs and dances to reinforce skills. The room slowly grew into an accepting focused learning environment where students relied less on the instructor and became more self-confident to take learning risks or ask each other for assistance. Over time, a robust academic focus replaced anger and negative attitudes. We started having more good days and less challenging ones. A few weeks into the semester, I was less doubtful of my abilities and gaining more confidence in theirs. We were all evolving.

Academic performance and social behaviors trended upwards. I wondered if it was time to test my students' behaviors by associating with others. The answer came quickly. We started to get compliments about improved behaviors from the principal and other teachers, which helped to boost confidence and self-esteem. I started to share progress reports with the principal.

Another big win was that parents began to respond and show up more regularly for parent-teacher meetings. Transferring to middle school made this an important year. The number one goal was to help my twelve students finish the year more successfully than how it began. Graduation was imminent, so I got involved in planning and organizing their moving-up ceremonies.

In the end, all twelve students achieved significantly. While there was still work to be done, there were no retentions. Throughout that year, I regularly assessed and monitored my instructional practices against my students' test results. I was always cognizant of my attitude, words, and body language. A teacher sets the tone for the class. We all celebrated several essential firsts that year; there were no retentions, and I proudly and successfully completed my first teaching job in the United States.

At the end of that year, we all moved on. My second teaching experience provided similar levels of satisfaction and rewards, but in different ways. I moved to another state and into a third-grade classroom with students who, unlike my sixth-grade students, generally experienced school success. Parents were extremely engaged in school activities. Ample volunteers helped with daily classroom activities.

Student whose disciplinary issues were minimal also grasped new information quickly, which allowed extra time for extended activities like performing modified versions of Shakespearean plays or proudly presenting custom-made plays on the cafeteria stage for other classes and for families.

In America, each state has unique teaching requirements, rules, and regulations. So, I once again found myself on a huge learning curve. Knowing that my success would cascade into success for students, I asked many questions of others and myself, sought help, established mentors, and developed relationships. Before long, I assimilated and became one of the "star" teachers. Parents were extremely pleased with the progress children were making, and they expressed admiration and appreciation for the work I was doing. As a result, administrators received many requests from parents for students to be placed in my class.

Parents tend to form strong networks, so ideas spread about "good" and "bad" teachers, a criterion mainly based on feelings and word of mouth, not necessarily data. Unfortunately, such behaviors create one more layer of scrutiny for teachers.

Teachers, like mothers, have eyes in the backs of their heads. I knew that my coworkers, for the most part, also evaluated the strengths and weaknesses of their peers. Based on my students' achievements and my participation in faculty discussions and willingness to learn, my coworkers recruited me to join various school-based committees.

I lead a school-based committee tasked with analyzing teaching and learning across the school and to develop an action plan for improvement. We developed and implemented a comprehensive school-wide reform initiative called Continuous Improvement Model. The entire school was organized into three main groupings as opposed to traditional age or specific grade levels. Kindergarten and first, second, third, fourth, and fifth were renamed alpha, beta, and omega, respectively. Each group of students remained with the same teacher for two consecutive years.

An outcome from implementing the initiative was teaching and learning should not have grade-specific start and end time but should provide learning and development opportunities with the same teacher and classmates for an extended period. For students whose learning style was not compatible with the newly created Continuous Improvement Model, at least one typical grade-specific class remained at each level for kindergarten through fifth.

The entire staff worked hard to implement the data-driven initiative as designed, and we were successful. Most students improved, and an additional benefit was the increased collaboration between and among faculty and staff. Parents loved the continuity for children. On my self-improvement track, I saw a need to examine and expand my collaborative skills, to develop more patience, to work with my team to monitor student progress consistently, and to adjust instruction vigorously to maximize learning. I gradually became a teacher leader, gaining the respect of my peers, school administrators, and unknowingly prominent people at the central office level.

As my pedagogy improved, so did my confidence, resulting in a lively nontraditional child-centered classroom where students sat in groups, worked and made decisions collaboratively, and planned theme-based projects like using Legos and artistic skills to create a future city. The projects enhanced curriculum topics and learning skills. When we studied about people and places, relevant extensions to lessons was sometime preparing a food unique to the region. We were the only classroom equipped with a conventional microwave oven and side-by-side refrigerator, which were donated by a parent.

The unconventional classroom setting generated publicity. We made a few appearances on local television news. The school district showcased our class as a model for best practices to an extent that we were featured in two nationwide teacher recruitment videos.

The daily motivation in the class was a teacher's dream. The eagerness and excitement were reciprocated. No two days were the same, for a discussion, an assignment, or news item would precipitate ideas for upcoming activities like a field trip. One year we went on twenty-five field trips, visiting art and science museums as well as botanical gardens, also watching plays and performances in theaters. The third-grade reading textbook had a story about the sport of jai alai. To make this content real for students, I contacted a local jai alai arena, and they arranged a game just for us. Children should know that a significant part of learning happens outside of the classroom, through people, places, and events within the community. I was learning alongside my students.

Another great memory was the time we entered the student media animation contest and our class placed first, second, and third in all categories. The entire class attended the award ceremony. Irrespective of the size and role a student played preparing for the competition, every student went on stage to accept the trophies. These activities, never done in isolation, were always accompanied by appropriate lesson plans complete with learning outcomes and assessments and still aligned with the established curriculum standards. I always checked to make sure I was meeting required state and local student and teacher expectations.

The principal was my biggest cheerleader, recognizing my willingness to identify students' needs and to develop individualized strategies accordingly. Even though I had no formal training in gifted education, the school leader trusted my abilities and assigned me to teach gifted students. To develop additional skills for the new assignment, I voluntarily enrolled in classes to enhance my knowledge and skills in gifted education.

Never was my ability to assess a situation and develop a plan of action more important than when I became principal of an elementary school located in the southeastern United States. The neighborhood school was listed amongst the oldest in the district and served about seven hundred kindergarteners through fifth-grade children. The majority of students walked to school, a few rode bikes, and a handful were driven by parents or community childcare agencies.

The school received a large federal education grant to fund a fine arts magnet program that retrofitted the facilities to accommodate performing and visual arts activities. The goals for the program were to provide a unique learning opportunity for students, to integrate the student population, and to improve academic achievement. In addition to the requirements of the core curriculum subjects of language arts (reading, writing, listening, speaking, and viewing), mathematics, science, and social studies, all students were required to participate in approximately one and a half hours of performing and visual arts or arts-related daily activities. The school got permission to have an extended school day.

The school had traditional personnel staffing, with administrative and instructional staff. Moreover, some of the fifty-seven teachers specialized in the arts. Written into the grant was a significant number of teachers' aides and an additional school counselor who served to expand the instructional and support team. Although additional funding for personnel and elaborate materials and equipment were in abundance, the school's performance on statewide assessment was depressing.

The state report showed that school grades and student scores had been showing a downward trend over time. There was a decline in enrollment of Caucasian students, an increase of black students, and no significant changes in the number of Hispanic students. The poverty rate was increasing. The absentee rate fluctuated. Both the Limited English Proficient (LEP) and Exceptional Student Education (ESE) student populations were steadily rising. Student discipline infractions were not proportionate for a school of approximately seven hundred students. The data also showed that parent and community participation and involvement were relatively low. Also reported were individual teacher effectiveness data that matched student performance. Student and teacher attendance patterns—and sadly, the recently initiated arts magnet program—showed marginal impact on academic achievement, attendance, or integration.

After examining the school's data, my next task was examining out-of-school influences like community engagement, socioeconomic status of families and students, and family support systems. I first went to the city's website for information. In addition to the usual demographic and governmental information, the site highlighted pictures showing the energetic spirit of the town, which hosted events like an annual garlic festival, the decorating and lighting of one of the tallest Christmas trees in the nation, and the coming together of a community on First Night, January 1. I traveled the neighborhood at different times of the day. I read police reports about arrests. Incidents of illegal substances haunted the neighborhood that included the school's surroundings. Burglaries and school break-ins and, frighteningly, vandalism of teachers' vehicles were glaring.

I was overwhelmed with the negative information and perplexed about the mammoth task it would take to make a difference in the school. The negatives outweighed the positives. I constantly replayed the disheartening data in my head. However, my conviction that all children deserve a high-quality education with opportunities to develop and grow remained forefront. All children deserve to be in schools where they feel physically safe and comfortable taking academic risks. I believe that places of learning should help students accept failure as part of the process to learn and grow and not as an excuse to stop trying or to give up. Importantly, I affirm that children belong in schools and classrooms with adults who trust, understand, and believe in them. Teachers should wholeheartedly have confidence in their abilities to make a positive difference in the cognitive and affective development of each child.

As leader responsible for students and staff, I experienced many emotions, scared for our safety in a community that had overwhelming crime. Despite the worrisome moments, I grew excited about the school's potential and the opportunities of making a significant difference in the school and community. Occassionally, I questioned if I should undertake the risks and challenges involved in leading a school with obvious insurmountable odds. Plus, concerns about the inevitable sacrifices like giving up time with family and friends. I fought the on and off flight-or-fight response floating through my head. Despite the back-and-forth, I was committed. Where should I begin? I decided to draw on years of research of best practices to get going.

I started by assembling a team along with additional support for the school. I immediately reached out to the principal and fourth-grade teachers at a nearby high-achieving school who answered the call to assist with writing, which was one of the subjects on the statewide standardized test. The gracious neighbors read, scored, and gave feedback to our fourth-grade students and staff on writing assignments. Through the process, we evolved from being mere writing buddies to establishing sister school relationships and sharing professional ideas and camaraderie. At year's end, when we achieved our first ever A grade, the sister school's response was heartfelt, taking pride in their role and being genuinely happy for our historic accomplishment. Throughout this book, I will refer to this school as the turnaround school.

Over my career, I learned the importance of taking personal inventories and sharpening my skills to advance my education and to grasp opportunities that invariably had far-reaching benefits for my students. Students' successes enhanced my personal and professional development. I became the first black assistant principal in a majority Caucasian school and community. When I was a little girl, my aspiration was to be a caring teacher like my teachers. Back then, I never dreamt of becoming the first Jamaican-born principal in a school district in the United States of America. Neither could I have envisioned being the first Jamaican-born assistant superintendent. Today I look with awe at my numerous awards and recognitions. I know that allowing me to be vulnerable with self-examination, looking at ways to improve my craft and my attitude and taking responsibilities for student achievement and school improvement, created a win-win situation.

Teachers' Corner

1. Have you ever intentionally assessed the impact of your daily instruction? What did you learn? How did you use the results?

2. Have you ever asked a peer to observe you teaching and provide feedback? If so, what did you do with the constructive criticism? If not, try it.

3. Teachers face continuous evaluation by students, parents, supervisors, and results from both state and federal assessments. How comfortable are you in your abilities to not be deterred by ongoing scrutiny? How do you know?

4. Students sometimes perform below expectations. How do you respond when students fail?

5. How do you assess your fitness for duty?

6. Have you ever asked your students to provide you with feedback on your teaching? If no, try it.

7. Describe a challenging school environment. Have you ever taught in such a school? How did you help change the situation?

8. If you were asked to fix your school, what steps would you take? How would the change look?

9. When did you last volunteer to participate in or lead a professional development session? What was the topic or focus? Why and how did you choose the focus of study?

10. A school environment should be conducive to teaching and learning. Other than your teaching responsibilities, how do you contribute to making your school a place you would send your child?

Digging In

1. Gather a group of staff members whose goal is to support new teachers to the school or the profession. Along with the new teacher, brainstorm topics for discussion. Encourage the experienced teacher to visit classrooms of veteran educators to observe teaching practices. Similarly, the new teacher may invite members of the group to observe her class, provide informal feedback, and give help as needed.

2. At the beginning of each week, help students develop individual and group goals. Throughout the week, monitor progress toward learning and behavior goals. At the end of the week, assess whether established goals were met, analyze results, and celebrate success. Make necessary adjustments.

3. Work with students to brainstorm ways to celebrate achievements. Activities may include supervised free time, ice cream parties, board games hour and free reading time from books chosen by students.

4. Work with school administrators to develop a school-wide needs assessment survey that includes examining student and teacher performance data. Ask open-ended questions centered on topics like school operations and morale. Analyze survey results, share with all stakeholders, and develop a realistic action plan.

5. Each school year identify places and events (science museum, theater, art gallery) outside of school, which can extend learning and enhance the curriculum. Before the visit, prepare students. Teach relevant vocabulary words, assign research activities, and possibly get an expert guest speaker. The more information

students have, the more enriching will be the visit. After the field trip, have students make journal entries of the experience, share, and use the compositions as a reading activity and/or discussion. For students who cannot afford the costs associated with field trips, establish a field trip fund and ask other parents or community representatives to contribute. Work with the school cafeteria to sponsor meals.

3

Test

TEACHERS ARE REQUIRED TO EVALUATE STUDENTS REGularly. Data collected is used to ascertain areas of strength, analyze weaknesses, and develop plans for growth. Despite the additional work on the educator's part or the students' discomfort from continuous assessments, the results are needed to inform instruction. Of course, students are not the only ones to face ongoing evaluations. Teachers, for the most part, are relatively comfortable with protocols, preparation for and administering assessments to students. While anxious about what tests will reveal, teachers use the information to guide instruction. However, when it comes to examining oneself or being judged by others, as stated in the previous chapter, formal evaluation takes on a whole different meaning. We tend to be our worst critics.

I know few teachers who get excited to be formally evaluated. For the majority, a myriad of emotions set in. For some, worrying begins when the official evaluation notice is posted. Some persons stress about the possibility of not remembering the information to be covered or the procedures to follow. Still others get anxious about the aesthetics of the classroom and nervously check and recheck to ensure there are no lopsided charts on the walls and that all desks and chairs are clean and neatly in place. Occasionally, divine intervention is silently requested, hoping that little Johnny does not have one of his incredible outbursts and that all students will be polite and actively participate. Any comment made by the observer is subjected to overthinking and overanalyzing, which contributes to stressors associated with assessment and evaluations.

Anxiety sometimes overshadows rational thinking, and we tend to forget the real purpose for evaluations. As a young teacher, I was 100 percent in the worrying and anxiety categories, both leading up to the moment while I waited for feedback and then hanging on to every word shared by the evaluator.

I finally decided to take steps to overcome the apprehensions. Looking at previous evaluations and comments and examining students' state assessment data was a great start. Then getting help is always beneficial. Whether I was in a small or large school setting, I always had the pleasure of the principal conducting my observation. Therefore, I sought assistance of other persons in leadership or reached out to one of my peers to do pre-observation of my teaching and provide objective feedback. The positive comments boosted my confidence. While I was not always happy to get "needs improvement" comments, the information provided an opportunity to learn and fix any problem areas before the real observation. While the approach to seeking help may contribute to some vulnerability, I usually felt more prepared and less anxious about the formal evaluation process.

Another helpful activity that required more planning and coordination was to videotape my teaching. Watching the tape allowed for objective critique and analysis of my behaviors, such as body language and interaction with students. I heard the tone of my voice, observed levels of students' responses, and received immediate impact of the lesson. At times, I made audio recordings. Today, with the popularity of smartphones, it is easier to make different types of recordings to capture a lesson. Improvement for both students and teacher comes in listening critically, doing self-analysis, and then researching ways to do better.

When I taught older students, I developed the courage to have them provide feedback on my teaching performance. This approach can be intimidating because students tend to be brutally honest. However, it was an opportunity to assess my performance through the eyes of learners and make needed changes. To get feedback from younger students, at the end of each lesson, I asked leading questions to get reaction about sections of, or the entire class session, about materials and equipment used and how students felt and responded during and after the lesson. Responses provided insight into content covered. Again, the feedback was not always positive, but the primary goal of assessment is to get a sense of strengths and weaknesses geared toward successful outcomes for both students and instructor.

I strongly believe that taking a closer look at teaching performance will reveal more than content knowledge and how it is delivered. I got to observe my tolerance, patience, and my energy level. I also learned to laugh at myself and laugh with my students to relax more into the job. As a result, I decided to have fun, which lowered my anxiety. The more composed the teacher, the calmer the classroom and the more receptive students will be to learn.

On a side note, people tend to make decisions and arrive at conclusions based on personal experiences. The more we learn about ourselves, the more in tune we become to understanding how and why we respond and behave in specific ways. Teachers must take the time to delve into how they react and become aware of the impact to students. Additionally, we must be mindful of the influence of our beliefs on developing minds we encounter in classrooms year after year. We are role models, and our students watch every move and hang on to every word uttered.

Throughout my forty-year career, I was fortunate to get opportunities that bolstered my successful climb up the career ladder from classroom teacher through to senior leadership in the central office. My advancements were possible because I took the time to assess my preparedness and readiness for different jobs. The approach of knowing, preparing, and valuing my worth significantly contributed to a successful career and family life. Knowledge is power, which strengthens confidence.

Teacher collaboration is another approach to assessing instructional strengths and weaknesses. When I was a principal, it was my practice to engage all teachers in weekly group planning geared exclusively on students' academic and behavioral progress. At each meeting, teachers brought samples of students' work, weekly test results, documentation of observable behaviors, and all issues that impacted student achievement throughout that week. Ongoing discussions and cooperative planning served multiple purposes: increase in trust levels that over time led to vibrant and respectful discourse and solutions to problems as opposed to passing around blame.

The sessions did more than enhance teaching and learning. Teachers learned firsthand about the abilities of their peers, identified individuals to serve as an additional resource, and highlighted anyone who may need additional support and encouragement. The teacher-led meetings helped to lower anxieties, especially around the subject of evaluation and related stress factors.

We do not always win at everything we do, but progress happens when we learn from our successes as well as our failures. Whether I was sitting in the teacher's or principal's chair at the end of each day, I would engage in self-reflection. Retrospection pinpointed areas deserving of a pat on the back as well as underscored areas to fix. Personal reflection was especially helpful following critical meetings with parents, staff, or students. If the session was a mutual win, I applauded myself. If not, I would try to make corrections plus work not to repeat any mistakes I made.

I believe there are long-term advantages for students when they too are taught how to self-assess. First is the value of enhanced engagement in learning. Second, in reflecting, students learn the rewards of setting goals, whether it is for academic or personal success. Third, the approach helps reduce or eliminate angsts associated with assessments. To show students the usefulness of ongoing self-assessment, one strategy I implemented was to have pupils graph academic progress over a specified period—one or more weeks, depending on the scope of what they were studying. The simple graphs showed weekly progress toward standard or learning targets in one or all subject areas. I placed more emphasis on reading, writing, and mathematics, which at the time were the subjects addressed on the state test. The colorful visual provided immediate feedback and was a springboard for enhancement or remediation activities. Another advantage was the sense of satisfaction that no matter results of the formative tests, ongoing help and support were guaranteed.

Another activity was the development and use of scoring rubrics to evaluate hands-on projects or essays. My experience has shown that when students are aware of the specific criteria for judging a completed assignment, chances are they will work more purposefully and confidently. Rubrics help students take ownership and become engaged in learning, ultimately leading to successful outcomes.

My experiences have also shown that some people who avoid taking steps to know their strengths and weaknesses are usually reluctant or afraid to see what results will unravel. While I too have moments of doubt, I also know that knowledge can be empowering and liberating.

People respond differently to assessment results. No one likes to get an F rating because of the stigma associated with failure, plus the personal feelings of unworthiness, embarrassments, defeats, and disappointments. For those reasons, some grown-ups may feel trapped, overwhelmed, and afraid to venture out, to try new things and to make important decisions, fearing the unknown. The idea of failing has negative consequences on young children as well. Lack of the appropriate words to use and acceptable ways to express emotions about repeated academic disappointments sometimes leads to anger and outbursts. Some students go in shutdown mode, yet those with grit and determination develop strategies to overcome and improve.

It is critical for teachers to examine their attitudes and anxieties about testing and assessment to ensure that students are getting positive verbal and nonverbal messages. Whether we like it or not, assessment will always be part of the political narrative in education, especially how public funds are expended. I have proven that focus on the advantages rather than on the disadvantages of testing, observations, and overall evaluations will help save us from sleepless nights and unwanted distresses.

Teachers' Corner

1. Identify connections between your personal and professional life. What are they? How do you know? Which aspects of the link are more influential?

2. Do you believe some teachers are misplaced? Without using names, please provide reasons for your answer and include possible ways to handle the situation.

3. What are your thoughts on the teacher evaluation system used in your school?

4. If you were asked to design a teacher evaluation system, what components would you include? How would you use the tool?

5. Do you think students are tested excessively? If so, suggest solutions or alternatives.

6. What are your thoughts on students evaluating teachers?

7. Do you engage in self-evaluations? What systems do you use? How do you handle the results?

8. How do you know when you are teaching the right grade or subject?

9. Is teaching the profession for you? How do you know?

10. Reflect on your value system. Is it leading you to career success?

Digging In

1. Research free career and personal assessment tools. Identify one that suits your needs. Take the survey, be honest with yourself about the results, and develop plans for improvement.

2. Place a comment box in your classroom or office. Encourage and give students opportunities to write anonymous feedback on lessons, your teaching, or the climate of the environment. Clear the box weekly, be receptive to the comments, and commit to making changes or providing explanations.

3. To prepare for career advancements, take advantage of varied professional and personal growth opportunities. Participate in workshops and training beyond the required. Study for advanced degrees. Ask for permission to share new information with coworkers.

4. Along with students, design a student evaluation form. To help students in the development of the document, provide example questions such as the following.

    - How do you think you did on …?
    - How could you have done better?
    - What kind of help do you think you need?
    - Who do you think can help you improve?

Whenever possible, provide students with a rubric that outlines evaluation of assignments. The grading criteria remove the mystery about assignment expectations and will improve student performance.

4

Confront Your Truth

FOR YEARS, I WAS A DEDICATED WALKER, TREKKING three and a half miles at least five days per week in the warm Florida sun. To support my health and wellness goals, I take great pride in making healthy food choices most of the time, not counting my trip to Italy and gourmandizing on gelato. I was proud of my exercise routine and eating habits and readily bragged to anyone who would listen. I convinced myself that my food and workout practices would result in significant weight loss and maintenance. Unfortunately, expectations did not match results.

Faced with a weight dilemma, I had three options: continue the same path, quit, or make realistic modifications. I chose the latter and added weight-bearing exercises to my routine. To make that decision, I first had to face the truth that what I was doing was not working. The next step was to devise a practical and realistic plan geared toward remedying the situation. The process was a simple equation of recognizing and owning a problem, formulating and faithfully implementing a plan of action. As I worked on improving my health, I realized that the formula is transferable and applicable to life, including the workplace, school, and within families.

If we accept the premise that the most significant variable to student achievement is effective instruction, we must admit that some strategies in schools are not working. Most teachers go beyond the call of duty to find ways to enhance student success. A significant few readily place blame on others and sometimes even on inanimate objects like the furniture and the age of the school building rather than examining the situation and sharing in the responsibility and resolution.

In my book *7 Insider Secrets: Transform Your Low-Performing Elementary School and Score an "A" in Record Time* (Cover 2013), I described teachers who had difficulties accepting any role and responsibilities for students' academic performance. My first task at that school was to analyze student data. It was important to have baseline information to decide on an action plan. I also encouraged teachers to complete an anonymous survey that included perspectives for lagging student performance.

Responses included need for more autonomy over teaching practices; poverty negatively impacted learning, discipline problems, and paltry consequences were getting in the way of teaching and learning, fingers pointed to administration and poor parenting and, shockingly, the physical arrangement of classroom furniture. Rather than traditional single desks in straight rows, students sat at oval-shaped tables with up to five chairs, allowing for ongoing cooperative learning and collaboration, strategies supported by research. Interestingly, no survey response suggested adding professional development to improve areas of deficiencies. Nor was there willingness to try different approaches to improve student achievement.

Think back to times in college when you took a test or exam and believed that you performed horribly. While waiting for the results, nagging worries of failure and its consequences continuously crept into your thoughts, immediately followed by rapid heartbeats and sweaty palms. In my head, a low score meant unworthiness and was a poor reflection of my character and my abilities. Over time, I managed to overcome the gripping fear and acknowledged that seeking help through tutoring or joining a study group would be helpful. Sometimes educators must take students by the hand to help them overcome the fear of failure and identify how to get help.

Forty years ago, I migrated from Jamaica with my husband and two small children in pursuit of educational and job opportunities in the United States of America. Since then, I have gone through many changes; however, to date, that move to a different country has been my most challenging undertaking. We moved far away from family and friends, a culture with practices and customs we adore, a support team that showed up before we called for help, and a carefree lifestyle. Assimilation into a foreign country was much harder than I anticipated.

Etched in my memory are Sunday walks along the beach or falling asleep to soothing sounds of waves teasing the shoreline and then slowly making their way back to the beautiful blue ocean. My beachside slumber would be interrupted by a fisherman selling fresh catch, my stomach wanting food or my subconscious telling me it was time to go home. Family vacations to luxurious resorts were now impossible. Sadly, Mama and extended family members were thousands of miles away, not accessible by car, and phone calls were unaffordable. Worse, we barely had enough money to get by.

The absence of Jamaican cuisine elevated my stress level and daily frustrations. Just about everything was new and intimidating. I remember getting grapes in the grocery store, and by the time I got to the cashier, I had lost some through holes in the shopping cart. I never realized bags were provided for produce. At first, I had difficulties understanding cultural context in conversations, so I either tried to use context clues or embarrassingly slowed the flow of conversation to ask for explanations. Sometimes I felt like a kindergartner transitioning from a non–English-speaking country and assimilating into the American school and life in general.

My source of income was unskilled low-paying jobs in retail stores, with weekly changes in my schedule and working long hours, sometimes without breaks. My work life was challenging for me and extremely burdensome for my family. The experience made me more empathetic when I later started to work in schools with students from foreign lands who sit in classrooms trying to learn, adjusting to a new life, and those old enough worrying about and watching parents struggle to make a new life.

The truth is that our situation was bleak, but my husband and I protected our young kids from the sadness. It is parents' responsibilities to provide food, shelter, and clothing, so there was little time to wallow in self-pity. Activities like dinner dates and taking the kids to amusement parks and museums were luxuries we could not afford. However, I got up each day and made a conscious effort to move forward, even though I sometimes felt like the situation had won the battle.

The fact is, I moved to the country to further my education. Too tired to fall asleep some nights, I lay in bed thinking about my teaching career and how far away it seemed. While I worked extremely hard at being the best cashier or award-winning salesperson, my passion was to teach, and I longed for the day to be back in the classroom doing what I love. The defining moment came when I asked myself the question "What are you doing about this?" ("Once a teacher, always a teacher.") The life I was living was not the one I envisioned for myself and family, so I paid a visit to the local school district's personnel office. I knew the Jamaican teaching credentials I had were different from the district's requirements, but I went, cautiously optimistic for the opportunity to resume teaching while simultaneously taking the necessary coursework. Why did I think the hiring rules and teaching requirements would be modified to meet my desperate needs?

I was devastated to learn that my certificate only met the requirements of a teacher's aide and I still needed to pass a spelling test to qualify for the job. My heart sank. I stood speechless as the words "teacher's aide" played repeatedly in my head. I thought about my children, the big dreams for our family that initially inspired our migration, and my silent distress at doing odd jobs. Disappointed yet optimistic, I agreed to take the spelling test. My perfect score, not surprising to me, visibly shocked my evaluator, who obviously underestimated my abilities.

To this day, whenever I find myself rushing to judgment about a person or situation, I am reminded to get as many facts as possible before deciding. Also, a reminder to teachers: never size up a student's aptitude based on initial appearance.

I believe the evaluator's reaction hurt more than my thinking about working as an aide. Suddenly, I was overcome with emotions and hurried from the building. All pent-up emotions associated with homesickness, lack of career focus, and challenges associated with financial hardships took over. I was oblivious of onlookers staring at a grown woman bellowing and holding her gut. I made it to the car and eventually pulled myself together. I dried my tears, reminded myself of the dream, and asked my husband to drive to Louisiana

State University. He was still in shock with my crying and my surprise desire to go to the university, but he straightened up, took the wheel, and cautiously drove as requested. Less than one year after that emotional outburst and breakthrough, I began the process to become a teacher.

As I walked across the stage on graduation day two years later, happy tears streamed down my face. To top it off, I immediately accepted a sixth-grade teaching job at the elementary school where I completed my internship course. Confronting my truth gave me a kick-start, not to mention the overall improvement to our family's standard of living.

The more teachers know about the backgrounds from which students come, chances are that classroom instructions and activities will be tailored to meet academic needs. As a classroom teacher, I had regular conferences with each child's parent. The ongoing dialogue between home and school was mutually beneficial. Parents knew the academic and behavioral expectations and understood how to provide support at home. I believe that strong partnerships break down potential barriers as well as improve trust and strengthen accountability, a great recipe for school success. Knowing this, a strategy in my successful school reform model was to require teachers to conduct home visits. The plan was initially unfavorable; however, after the benefits became obvious, the resistance diminished and by midyear, home visits were no longer an issue.

At my turnaround school, data showed a need to improve classroom instruction. Despite pertinent professional development and countless classroom observations with immediate feedback and follow-up visits, little changed in classroom instruction. With need for drastic academic improvement, I concluded that changes in teaching staff were necessary. The decision made, in the best interest of children, had the perception of unfairness to teachers who vocalized hurt and disappointment in the decision. The teacher in me felt perturbed about having to make drastic personnel decisions. However, I negotiated with my supervisors that each impacted person would be guaranteed a job elsewhere in the school district. In the end, an instructional overhaul proved valuable to student achievement and school improvement.

It is helpful for students to be aware of and to be able to verbalize and importantly confront fears associated with school performance. An activity I frequently use to help students minimize anxieties is through writing. One assignment required writing a letter to share thoughts on fears of testing. The letter addressed to themselves must be specific about concerns, where to get help, and how to outline a plan of action to combat testing jitters. The strategy not only helps students reduce worrying but also reassures them that they have the ability and skills to succeed.

Along the same lines, in preparing students for high-stakes standardized tests, students got opportunities to verbalize different scenarios, with solutions, should test results prove unfavorable. Faced with alternatives, students tend to approach testing more relaxed, hence focusing on the exam and less on the outcome.

Irrespective of one's place in life, facing our truths is never easy. Various tactics are employed to deal with issues: implementing avoidance tactics, blame shifting, pretending the problems don't exist, wishing issues would disappear, and getting someone else to be the fixer or confront the situation.

Eventually, we must deal with realities. even though the process can be hurtful. However, the examination of our actions, thoughts, and behaviors is liberating. The process clears the way for clear thoughts and healthy decision-making, with potential to explore opportunities for change and growth. Using data, teachers can help students recognize strengths and weaknesses and then design a realistic action plan.

Whatever your pursuits, aspirations, or desires, they should begin with a quest for the truth, which will, in the end, help to pave the way for authenticity and peace of mind.

Teachers' Corner

1. My truth is that I was born to teach. Are you living your professional truth?

2. How do you encourage individuality within your classroom community?

3. Have you ever paused and taken time to truly understand who you are? What did you do?

4. Teaching is hard work. What keeps you motivated?

5. If you had a choice of another profession, which one would you choose? Why?

6. List ten things that you believe to be true about children.

7. Would you hire you to teach? If so, why?

8. What are your deepest fears and doubts about teaching?

9. What subject do you most like or dislike to teach? Why?

10. If you could restart your career journey, would you still become a teacher? If so, why?

Digging In

1. Every school has teachers who blame a student for poor academic performance and progress. The blamers are usually individuals who sit on the fringe in the back of the room during faculty meetings, taking a wait-and-see attitude, and are usually the last to volunteer, if ever, for school activities, and whose words and body language scream negativity. To bring the outliers gradually into the mainstream, have regular meetings specifically to provide an outlet for their frustrations and input. Whenever possible, request the naysayers to share valid and reliable data to corroborate point of view. Faced with the truth, most cynics will either adjust their views or be open to listening.

2. Have one-to-one data chats with students. Compare past and current data and develop specific plans for improvement. When appropriate, invite parents to meetings and have students lead the data conversation and action strategies.

3. Have students read and share biographies about people who faced the stark reality of their situation and adjusted, resulting in personal or professional improvement.

4. Identify the lowest performing students in your school. Research, develop and implement a strategic academic action plan. Include monitoring strategies and create room for adjustments.

5. If analyzing data is a weakness in your school or department, find related and appropriate professional development focused on the topic. If there is no data or curriculum team in your school, work with the school's administration to create one.

5

Communicate to Elevate

EFFECTIVE COMMUNICATION IS CRITICAL FOR EVERYONE, more so for educators. Teaching requires daily interactions with various stakeholders—children and families, coworkers and supervisors, ancillary workers, community representatives, and child advocates, just to name a few. The verbal and nonverbal messages we convey speak volumes about our character and deportment, show personal feelings for the listening or viewing audience, and help others form opinions about us.

Student academic success hinges on the quality, relevance, and efficient delivery of instruction. Connecting with students is the first step, despite barriers like personal experiences, personalities, and idiosyncrasies. Despite the potential obstacles, the adult in the room must initiate, foster, and maintain rapport with students. As a classroom teacher, I intentionally created opportunities for open dialogue with students. Some great moments included discussions about current events, holidays, and other topics to get everyone involved. Classroom rules, pop culture and celebrities, and making decisions on classroom projects always got most students' attention.

Obviously, nonverbal messages have the power to transmit empathy. My students and parents glowed when I attended sporting and other after-school events. Not only was I demonstrating that I care, but they also got a chance to see me in a less formal role. Sometimes I took my family along with me.

Each lesson in my class began with a brief, relevant, and captivating discussion. For example, a math class on money would be introduced with having several denominations of money and talking about real-world situations like purchasing goods and services, saving, and sharing—also deriving comfort from having extra cash on hand and a reason for effective management. Starting a debate by taking an unpopular position like saying "Children don't need free time in school" usually sparks interest and gets active participation.

Another opportunity to encourage communication was the ten-minute morning talk. Students took turns providing topics for the morning meetings that usually had everyone sitting in a circle. Not everyone shared every day, but before the week's end, any students who wished to express their opinions or feelings got a turn. Class discussions enhanced vocabulary and communication skills and importantly promoted respect for differing points of view. Among many positives, open and authentic dialogues showed students that I was interested in them and what they had to say, serving as another tool to bridge possible barriers like culture, race, and ethnicities.

At my acclaimed turnaround school, home visits proved beneficial to academic achievement and importantly served as a social bridge between home and school. Countless homeschool obstacles were broken down; teachers gained valuable insights about students' background, and over time, trust among all parties was established. In an external evaluation on the transformation project, both school staff and parents expressed the positive impact of the home visits.

As a college professor, I start out each class by posting expectations and objectives. I believe that establishing clear expectations with desired outcomes significantly contributes to student success, serves as a tremendous communication tool, and builds accountability. Over the years, students' evaluation of the course indicates that this strategy helped to establish expectations and to develop or improve study skills.

Teachers have unimaginable power to make or break a student's self-esteem through the climate established in the classroom, tone, type, immediacy of feedback, and another reminder: body language. Sometimes it is not so much about the words we use but instead how we use the words.

I learned early in my career that when students are actively engaged in learning and classroom operations, they take ownership and work hard for personal and group success. A process that generated discussion, excitement, and cooperation were establishing criteria to celebrate school and class success. My role in the discussions was to ensure that the rules set gave opportunities for all students to participate.

Every child in a classroom needs validation, which may be as informal as verbal compliments when one is caught doing well, making an effort, or showing appropriate behaviors. More formal and objective acknowledgments could include honoring academic achievement, validation of being on time, and attending school and participating in community activities like helping an elderly neighbor or tutoring a classmate.

Effective classroom communication also includes establishing fair and realistic class and school rules. The way infractions are handled makes a huge difference in the classroom climate. Students must face reprimands for inappropriate behaviors. A teacher's response to the situation will make all the difference. Refrain from engaging students in public confrontations, criticisms, and sarcasm—behaviors with the potential to escalate the situation and spawn fear.

Another approach to building bonds with students is sharing personal yet appropriate stories about pets, foods, children, siblings, and family trips. The stories may also communicate instances when the teacher made mistakes like putting on two different shoes or forgetting the packed lunch on the kitchen counter. When students see teachers' vulnerability, it sends a message that all humans blunder. Allowing students to see or hear about your mistakes and how you recover speaks volumes. Teachers impart much more than content knowledge and learning strategies.

Parents often complain that education language used in parent-teacher conferences is not easily understood, making it difficult for meaningful discourse. In meetings with parents, educators must use easy-to-understand words and phrases. For example, terminology used when sharing information about testing, special education laws, or legal mandates should be explained in layperson language. During the meeting, school staff should check for group understanding, provide language translators as needed, and give opportunities for the audience to ask questions.

I recently attended a school event and was disappointed to find grammatical and spelling errors in a published document. A gentle reminder is to solicit proofreading help and keep in mind that all communication is formal, and one never knows in whose hands the information may land or who may be listening.

Outside the classroom, a teacher's ability to communicate is paramount to personal and professional growth. Teachers often share that speaking with students is a no-brainer but addressing adult groups is a completely different situation. When I left the school center to work at the central office, I was occasionally tasked with presenting information to the school board. After preparing a speech or developing a PowerPoint presentation, I always solicited the help of proofreaders to look for typographical errors, determine whether the intended message was clear, and importantly, check my tone. Valuable resources are available to support persons who may get anxious about public speaking. As needed, get some tips and practice.

Teachers delight in advancing their education. Submitting college applications, writing essays, and communicating with professors are part of the process. In addition to adhering to general writing conventions, communicating ideas effectively is paramount to success.

Effective communication is critical in negotiations, sharing or soliciting valuable information, and establishing camaraderie and expectations. A breakdown in communication will lead to broken relationships and confusion in organizations, not to mention hampering success.

Teachers' Corner

1. List at least ten effective strategies geared toward building positive relationships with students, parents, coworkers, and members of the school community.

2. Describe five communication strategies to help students develop self-esteem. Please provide concrete implementation ideas.

3. How do you create a "family" atmosphere in your classroom?

4. Body language sometimes speaks louder than words. How do you monitor your body language?

5. What is your system for ensuring that you make daily contact with each student?

6. On a scale of one to ten, rate your ability to communicate efficiently. Please explain your response.

7. Actions speak louder than words. How does this relate to your interactions with your school community?

8. Describe an extracurricular event you attended to support a student. What were the reactions from the student or caregivers? How did you feel?

9. Are you a favorite teacher? How do you know?

10. Do you believe your tone needs adjustment? What is the proof? What steps will you take to change?

Digging In

1. If doing public speaking raises your blood pressure or anxiety levels, find and participate in a Toastmasters program or similar support services near you.

2. Be a continuous learner engaged in finding innovative strategies to enhance student learning. Often you will see very creative and useful approaches implemented in your school. However, taking time to attend conferences or conducting online research will also be valuable.

3. At least once per week, provide opportunities for students to talk. This scheduled activity may be student or teacher led, and both parties may choose topics for discussion. A suggestion box in the classroom for anonymous submittal may motivate participation.

4. Find out if your teacher contract approves home visits. Some parents will be more comfortable engaging in parent-teacher conferences held on their home turf. For some parents, home visits signify deep respect.

5. Invite a colleague to observe your class and provide feedback specifically on your verbal and nonverbal communication skills. Be sure to find an objective observer who will tell you the truth. Act on the recommendations.

6

Practice Healthy Habits

TEACHING IS NOT A WALK-IN-THE-PARK OCCUPATION. Most teachers assiduously prepare students every day for success, especially now with the significance of standardized tests, which include stringent rules and regulations as well as last-minute changes. Not to mention the distress associated with controversial teacher evaluation systems, limited autonomy to do the job for which they were trained, and added stressors dealing with student behavioral issues and too many asides unrelated to classroom instruction. With never-ending demands, there is no wonder more than half of the teaching workforce indicates a high degree of job-related tension.

Unchecked stress has negative consequences on our health and may lead to various physical ailments and illnesses, with potential to further advance increase anxiety and depression, contribute to related heart diseases, interrupt sleep, trigger weight problems, affect reasoning, slow productivity, and worse, possibly create destructive behaviors.

In our commitment to get the job done, prioritizing needs of others over our own and juggling demands for a work-life balance, we ignore vital body signs and symptoms and rarely pause to listen to what the body is saying until, sadly, sometimes it is too late. I write from personal experience. A few years ago, I woke up with what I thought was my usual migraine headache. After enduring the pain for a few days, I surrendered to the prescribed medication, which did little to ease the pain. However, I kept pushing through, kidding myself that if I stayed focus and busy on my million and one tasks and assignments, the pain would eventually go away. Unfortunately, one week later I was in a comatose state in the hospital with a life-threatening diagnosis of thrombotic thrombocytopenic purpura (TTP) (Kuter 2019), a sporadic blood disorder. I avoided all the warning signs my body was sending and convinced myself I had no time to be sick; there was too much work to do. To the contrary, I ended up spending the entire summer in the hospital and at home recuperating, unable to help myself or anyone else. Luckily, I fully recovered from that severe illness.

That somber experience reminded me that I am not invincible, and while I love my job, family, and friends, it is critical that I maintain sound physical, mental, and social health. The ordeal also forced me to reevaluate and rethink my approach and actions relating to my health and well-being. A significant change I made was to take occasional time off from work without feeling guilty, enjoying pampering at a spa, inviting myself to a lovely lunch, or simply cherishing moments being a couch potato, reading fun materials or indulging in television shows that require very little or no thinking.

In this chapter, I am revisiting the concept of taking a self-inventory, but with emphasis on health and well-being. Whenever I begin to feel my energy level depleting or my disposition less than desirable, I take a breather and appraise the situation, starting with making a list to remind myself of the things that make me joyful and contented and then completing the activity by adding how often or if a recent engagement in any of the activities occurred. This visual aid, along with some soul-searching, often led me to make realistic and manageable changes. I also paused to take stock of the projects or tasks on which I had been working to determine if I had been overextending myself.

By nature, teachers are selfless, always overstretching themselves and making time to do one more thing for someone else, not wanting to turn anyone away. Giving to others is an admirable quality but should not be done at the expense of one's health and well-being. A simple way to overcome the desire of spreading yourself too thinly is by standing in front of the mirror and practice forming your lips to say the word *no*. The first time I refused to house a child in time-out was a personally daunting experiencing. I felt guilty and had to force myself from retracting. However, I offered to help provide the sending teacher with additional classroom management strategies. It took a while before I could make eye contact with my colleague. My momentary discomfort gave rise to a feeling of self-empowerment, which made it easier for me to say more nos.

For as long as I can remember, there has been a myth implying that teachers should know it all and have all the answers. With this pressure, many of my peers reluctantly sought personal or professional help for fear of being weak or ignorant. I internalized and perpetuated that falsehood. Maturity taught me otherwise. When I became a school principal, I purposefully established a school climate. I implemented collaborative team meetings and established a supportive work atmosphere that encouraged teachers to connect with their peers and others and not be embarrassed to ask for help. The notion of learning together made us all feel vulnerable and secure at the same time. I also provided fun activities at faculty meetings. In addition to dealing with the job-related tasks, I invited local massage therapists to give complimentary five-minute massages. It was common for me to personally prepare or have meals catered for teachers. Activities like these helped to minimize the day-to-day challenges of the job.

Teachers spend a great deal of time encouraging students to read for information and enjoyment, yet many do not take their own advice. With limited time, teachers tend to read only professional literature. Do you remember when we were children and our parents had to pry us away from books to encourage participation in activities like family dinners or, worse, to complete chores? Reading for pleasure is relaxing.

As a child, I was captivated by stories that took me on exotic excursions and sometimes into a land of make believe. That spurred my appetite to travel and got me curious about cultures and peoples. To think that I now live in a foreign land and have traveled to several countries.

I still love to read, even though listening to audiobooks as I travel is very convenient. However, I appreciate the quietness and calm reading affords and the opportunity to escape from life's challenges. As you focus on health and well-being, consider revisiting childhood practices that once brought joy and fulfillment; browse through old photo albums, walk in the park, visit family and friends, fix a favorite dish, go outdoors for the fun of it, play board games and assemble puzzles, watch funny movies, write letters, or send postcards. The list is endless. Do things that make you smile and warm your heart.

I am amazed at the unbelievable amount of work teachers accomplish during a thirty-minute lunch break. I recall checking my mailbox and responding to correspondences that always seemed urgent, returning phone calls, meeting with colleagues to develop strategies to help students, collecting and organizing materials and supplies for lessons—and still had about two minutes to gulp down lunch. The busyness of the day often spills over to after hours. Critical activities like grading papers and planning lessons, not included in the marathon lunch hour, typically secure a spot in the already overstuffed teacher bag for completion at home.

Once home, after tending to family responsibilities like cooking, paying bills, helping with homework, returning personal messages, checking on a sick neighbor or family member, doing grocery shopping, attention then turns to that overflowing briefcase. So limited time is left to relax and get adequate sleep. Despite widely shared research about the importance of a good night's sleep, educators tend to ignore the facts, with hope that one day things will improve.

Exercising, minimizing stress, and getting enough sleep are essential for the overall health of our bodies. Equally important is eating healthy. Educators, unfortunately, fall prey to poor eating habits, eating irregularly and not making time to plan meals but instead grabbing something to go or visiting the vending machine. I know this is true because of the countless times I failed miserably at trying to develop and maintain a healthier food and exercise regimen. It is difficult but necessary to cultivate healthful habits, especially with critical benefits like enhanced work efficiency, an improved frame of mind, and longevity. As a reminder, I must repeat what we have been repeatedly told: "We must first take care of self before taking care of others." Starting slowly and making gradual, sustainable changes have made the difference in my eating patterns, habits, and overall health.

"You cannot be both grateful and worried at the same time" is a mantra I use as a source of encouragement when I find myself slipping into melancholy. Over the years, I have learned that when I practice and express gratefulness, my attitude toward others and me improves. I feel at peace, become more optimistic about my life and career, and believe the experts who assert that enhanced physical health is a benefit of gratitude. I intentionally find ways each day to be grateful for the people in my life, my possessions, and the things I have accomplished.

So how do we encourage healthy habits in students? Make the time to teach about foods, model appropriate eating habits, include recess and downtime in daily activities, teach gratitude and respect, and provide an atmosphere for them to discuss issues of concern. I must hasten to say that student privacy is the law, so proceed with care.

Someone once told me that you appreciate your health more when you are sick. Illness can dampen dreams, minimize independence, drain finances, and impact socialization. It is critical to do everything in our power to model and practice healthy habits.

I have been an educator for approximately forty years, which means that I have former students who have completed college and are making a difference wherever they live and work. I feel enormous joy and happiness knowing that I played a small part in helping them shape their lives and possibly impact future generations. Most days I work on being happy!

Teachers' Corner

1. What do you do for fun?

2. Are you healthy? How do you know?

3. List five healthy habits you practice on a regular basis.

4. Are you happy with your life and career? Please explain.

5. When a current or past student expresses gratitude to you, how does it make you feel?

6. How do you encourage your students and coworkers to practice healthy habits?

7. List ten things and people for whom you are grateful.

8. List ten positive statements you hope to get from your students at the end of the school year.

9. What will the parents of your students say to you at the end of the school year?

10. On a scale of one to ten, how much do you love your profession? Please explain.

Digging In

1. Find a realistic food and exercise regimen to meet your personal and professional needs, consulting with a medical doctor before starting. Be true to the health goals established. Paying attention to your mental health is just as important as your physical health. I give you permission to take a day off occasionally and spend quality time with yourself. My day is usually on my birthday.

2. Stressful situations are part of living. Unpleasant parent-teacher conferences, getting negative feedback from a supervisor on recent classroom observation, sitting in heavy traffic, or having a disagreement with a loved one adds to the uneasiness. I recommend trying to pause before you speak or act; you may regret a hasty decision. The way you react could affect your health. Remember when mama used to tell us to think before we speak or take deep breaths and count to ten? Those words and suggestions still ring true today.

3. Expressions of gratitude help reduce stress. Keep a gratitude journal. Each day write at least seven things for which you are grateful. Encourage students to do the same.

4. If there are no safe avenues at your workplace for staff to share concerns, work with supervisors and a team of your peers to create an outlet. Hold publicly announced and regularly scheduled meetings that are transparent to all. Encourage contributions and participation from a cross section of the staff. Keep records of meetings to do a follow-up as needed. Likewise, have a box in the classroom or an accessible place in the school for students or others to share concerns anonymously.

5. Form a book club at work or within the community. Read a broad genre of literature. Meet outside of school, if possible, to conduct book talks. A change of venues like a local restaurant, coffee shop, or the public library will create a more social atmosphere and lessen the appearance of work. The benefits to morale and improved connectedness will be endless.

7

Set Goals

DETERMINATION, PERSEVERANCE, GRIT, AND MOTIVAtion are contributing factors to success. Whatever our age and status, success is possible with a vision and road map. Teaching is my calling, which has been the epicenter of my life since I was a little girl. Every significant personal and professional action on which I have embarked has been aligned with my aspirations.

Before the age of ten, I knew after high school graduation that my next step was to enroll in teacher's college. My support team, consisting of my immediate and extended family and teachers, knew and supported my plans. Later, anyone added to the circle joined the support team. For example, my fiancé knew that our wedding had to be during the summertime; that way I would not be absent from my students.

Although the resolve to set and realize goals can be excruciating, consistently having an action plan contributed significantly to my success and that of my hundreds of students. Completing grad school, managing a household, and working two jobs was no easy feat. When I was in graduate school, for example, I posted my yearly class schedule and related activities on the refrigerator door. The visual showed my short-term and long-term tasks as well as served as motivator for the entire family, who worked hard to organize important events like vacations and family events around my school and work schedules. Achieving my goals gave the entire family an uplift.

Leaders use goal-setting strategies to maintain organizational focus. Each year companies pay consultants to help employees develop goals to bolster morale or to increase profit.

When I was a classroom teacher, my daily lesson plans included outcomes for both student and teacher. With specific expectations that required students to give end-of-lesson feedback, I was able to measure my instruction's impact. Informal exit strategies included oral review questions or problem-solving activities posed by teacher or by learners. Individual lap chalkboards were frequently used to show responses. Feedback also helped to identify students needing additional educational support. Students used the question and answer period as a competition that improved listening skills and focus, especially during instruction.

A common characteristic among highly successful people is the ability to achieve goals. So each semester I teach my college freshmen the SMART (Smart Goals Guides 2018), This specific, measurable, attainable, realistic, and time-bound) format is a process that shows how to develop, employ, and monitor long-term and short-term objectives. Utilizing SMART (Smart Goals Guides 2018), strategies will enhance success for individuals and organizations. The goals are developed at the beginning of the term and are intermittently checked throughout the semester. Based on the desired outcomes, students create a vision board, which is a collection of pictures, photographs, and declarations of one's dreams, used as inspiration toward attaining goals. This activity gets positive reviews on course evaluation.

For years, I have maintained a pictorial as a visual to monitor my personal and professional progress. Most times I can check "achieved" and remove items from the board, sometimes items are marked "in progress," and it is not unusual for an indication of "deferred" to be assigned. I work at being realistic, not placing undue pressure on myself, although that is an untenable task.

A principal uses current and reliable data to establish individual, classroom, and schoolwide expectations. In previous chapters, I referenced my turnaround school. The mandate was for me to change the school's trajectory. The complexity of the school required an arduous process. Several strategies and programs were being implemented simultaneously, so a method for evaluating goals had to be established. In addition to modeling effective instructional leadership, I had to ensure that the processes in place were being implemented with fidelity. Weekly formative evaluations determined attainment of the short-term goals, while monthly summative assessments showed progress toward long-term goals.

As principal, I assigned myself the role of number one cheerleader. I set the tone and accepted responsibilities for school improvement. Each day I wore a tailor-made vest with a huge *A* on my chest and back, a constant reminder of the expected grade for the school. I monitored implementation of the rigorous curriculum, and all students were trained on "A" behaviors: completing all class and homework assignments, studying for tests, paying attention, and asking for help as often as needed. Parents knew the expectations and were invited to school regularly for parent meetings that included information on how they could support school activities.

Goal setting enhances accountability. Students were held responsible for learning. One very successful strategy was the 85 percent academic rule. Students were expected to score at least 85 percent on all school-developed assignments. In cases when the target was not met, automatic reteaching and retesting happened. This approach improved skills and self-esteem and importantly sent a message that failure can be fixed, and support is available.

Eventually, surpassing 85 percent became personal, class, and grade-level competitions. Even teachers got in the action. The healthy competition was electrifying. School and learning were obviously enjoyable.

It is evident that there is a correlation between goal setting, motivation, and success. My ability to create a vision for my life and students in my charge proved that success is not luck; it involves hard work, persistence, and a winning attitude. Learners of all ages, backgrounds, and abilities must be encouraged to tap into available resources at school, through school counselors, mentors, and academic advisors as well as places in the community like public libraries. Celebrating successes, big or small, must be embedded in a plan to achieve success.

Teachers' Corner

1. Define your personal and professional goals.

2. What is the difference between a dream and a goal?

3. List at least five strategies in place at your school to help students achieve and maintain academic goals.

4. If you have goals, chances are you will succeed. Do you agree? Please explain.

5. How do you include goal setting in your curriculum?

6. Describe your thoughts on the concept of "failure."

7. Describe a personal or professional goal you have accomplished. What is the significance?

8. How is risk-taking celebrated and encouraged in your classroom?

9. What does success look like to you? What does success mean to you?

10. Are you living your best life? How do you know?

Digging In

1. Specific, measurable, attainable, realistic, and time-bound (SMART), the goal-setting model, helps to guide development and attainment of long-term and short-term goals. Teach the SMART model, develop both academic and behavioral goals, and help students list members of a support team who will also serve as accountability partners.

2. Schedule a time every three to four months to evaluate and assess documented goals and make necessary adjustments.

3. A strategy to get immediate feedback on the effectiveness of a lesson is for teachers to list academic objectives on the whiteboard. The expected outcomes should be expressed in behavioral terms. For example, "Students will_____," thus enhancing accountability across the classroom community. Throughout the lesson, refer to the list to monitor for understanding. For lesson feedback, encourage students to write questions. This approach serves as reinforcement for students, while providing valuable instructional information to the teacher. Both teacher and students may ask open-ended exit questions. Students in cooperative groups may also design creative strategies to share what they learned from the lesson.

4. Daily teaching and learning goals should align with school, district, and state expectations. Therefore, every two or three-month, summative evaluations should be conducted to avoid any surprises or disappointments. Use results to celebrate achievements.

8

Maximize Learning

I GREW UP LEARNING THAT ONE IS NEVER TOO OLD TO learn. So, I am grateful to be in a profession that encourages professional development opportunities for its workforce. It is debatable whether the training received is timely, appropriate, or valuable for the audience. Despite swirling controversies, most educators I know welcome the chance to learn because to maintain success in any arena requires constant retooling.

Schools should not rely solely on local experts like teacher leaders and school district curriculum developers for professional development. National and international in-field masters help to broaden perspectives and provide information on the latest best practices in education. When I was a classroom teacher, I looked forward to faculty meetings where teachers shared effective strategies used in classrooms. In addition to boosting faculty morale, when teachers show successful approaches to their peers, it emphasizes potentials for other students within the school. Some of my most valuable learning experiences were at the National Association of Elementary School Principals, Council of the Great City Schools, and leadership seminars at both The Harvard Institute for School Leadership and at The Darden School of Executive Leadership Academy.

Using faculty meetings to share best practices is an efficient use of staff time, seizing opportunities with a captive audience. Observing each other's classrooms is another learning opportunity with an added benefit of creating a supportive and informed learning community.

As a school principal, it was my practice to spend more time in classrooms and work with students and staff rather than sitting at my desk. Yes, it meant more hours on the job after student- dismissal, but time spent impacting teaching and learning is worthwhile. Occasionally, I assumed responsibilities teaching a class, hiring substitute teachers to allow instructors to visit other classrooms or nearby schools to observe effective teaching strategies. Volunteering to teach also gave me opportunities to sharpen my instructional skills.

Training is also possible through group study. As a school leader, I was judicious with the school's budget. I prioritized students' and teachers' needs, purchasing books topical to school issues as identified by data yet inspiring to generate group study and enhance creativity. Some books focused on strategies to motivate reluctant and advanced learners, integrating arts into the curriculum, and teaching test-taking strategies.

Another training resource is active participation in subject area or grade-level team meetings. It was always gratifying to listen in on wholesome discussions centered on pedagogical strategies, student academic progress, and behaviors. The benefits are immeasurable. In addition to the impact on teaching and learning, meetings enhance leadership skills and highlight potential school administrators.

At times, I arranged for grade-level teachers to collaborate with counterparts in nearby schools for meaningful engagement in professional collaborations. Training sessions had agendas, outcomes, and plans for follow-up with small coequal teams. A usual takeaway is that children have common challenges irrespective of the school they attend and the backgrounds from which they come.

Teachers thrive in supportive school environments. I created a buddy system, a nonevaluative mentor or a team of persons with diverse skills to help new and inexperienced teachers or any teacher with a need. The teams were informal and helped to guide lesson planning, gave tips on how to handle off-task student behaviors, or simply offered shoulders at challenging moments. Both parties arranged mutually convenient meetings without input or involvement from the school's administration.

I attribute college education, complementary in-service training, and acquiring additional certifications for enhancing my opportunities for job advancements and positioning me as an in-field expert. When I was a classroom teacher, I availed myself of all possible personal and professional training and in-service activities as my schedule allowed. The school district website is a great resource to find trainings, as are professional journals and through networking with fellow educators. Teachers should also voice the need for additional training to the principal, who usually has a wealth of available information on conferences and workshops. A significant investment I made in my career was the decision to get a doctorate degree. It was taxing to juggle all my responsibilities. In the end, I increased my job prospects tenfold, respected for the ability to accomplish a significant goal, and was seen as being more credible.

I caution teachers to find balance between engaging in additional trainings, work responsibilities, and a social and family life. To confess, I sometimes never exercised equilibrium and experienced negative effects, as when there was not enough time for me to de-stress and rejuvenate, avoid intrusion on family time, and hamper social interactions, resulting in exhaustion and fatigue.

How thrilling is it to be considered an expert helping fellow educators resolve instructional and learning issues? On numerous occasions, I was invited to make presentations focused on topics like strategies that work, value of common assessments, improving school discipline, managing a school budget, impact of teacher collaboration, and winning turnaround strategies.

It is obvious that acquiring additional education and training made a difference in my career. I hope that this chapter helped to influence and support decisions for ongoing learning. Everyone is a winner, with high-quality, relevant, timely, and purposeful training and follow-up activities.

As Albert Einstein reminded us, intellectual growth should commence at birth and cease only at death.

Teachers' Corner

1. Describe the most valuable lesson you ever learned. How did the learning affect your life or work?

2. Share a professional development activity in which you participated within the last three months. How did you hear about the event? With whom did you share the information learned?

3. How would you like to change or improve your teaching? Where would you begin?

4. How would you like to change or improve your school? What are some beginning steps you will take?

5. Describe observable behaviors of a person who is continuously learning.

6. Suppose you have been commissioned to write and deliver a speech entitled "Learning Is Lifelong" to a graduating class. What would you say? Please list ten points.

7. What are you most passionate about? How will you maintain the interest for your passion?

8. Please share a lesson you learned from someone else's story. How will you use your life as a lesson to others?

9. How do you feel about being occasionally wrong or misguided? Identify a situation and the way you handled it.

10. List at least ten convincing reasons for ongoing training in the field of education.

Digging In

1. The results of assessments should drive professional development or other growth activities. Too often teachers are required to participate in training that is not compatible with current needs, often resulting in undue stress and frustrations and considered a waste of valuable time. After progress toward school goals are analyzed, conduct research to find the appropriate training to improve deficiencies. Start the search within the faculty. Teachers have a wealth of resources from which to draw. The school district website usually shares available training that is usually free to schools and delivered by individuals who have prior knowledge about your school and its environment. When funds are available, hiring a consultant for professional development is always an option. A consultant may present additional ideas from an objective perspective. Whatever source used or the purpose for training, I suggest that a team of people should be involved in the type and topics and create a plan to have multiple individuals cross-trained.

2. Participating in professional development to improve teaching and learning is critical, but just as important is training for personal growth and self-improvement. Participate in classes that focus on topics like stress and time management, how to set and achieve personal goals, and how to win at life in general.

3. At the end or beginning of each school year, a flexible training calendar should be developed, making room for additional activities as needs arise. The entire staff should be involved in creating a functioning training schedule. By so doing, buy-in will be easier and the development needs of students and staff addressed.

4. I believe in ongoing student training around behavioral expectations. Enforce punishment only after students learn class and school rules. What are your thoughts?

5. More mature pupils should have input for extracurricular opportunities. For example, clubs that focus on specific subject areas like science and horticulture, dance and music, or civic engagement, like the Key Club. Involvement in such activities creates a sense of community, enhances leadership and social skills, and develops discipline and responsibility.

9

Do Without

"IF YOU WANT GOOD, YOUR NOSE MUST RUN" (HARRIS 2002, 61). This quote in Jamaican *patois* translated means "to accomplish certain things, you have to sacrifice." This and countless other adages, passed down through generations, served to inspire, keep us safe, and reinforce cultural norms while providing rules to guide future generations. Another favorite that Mama drilled and that I too have taught my three children is "The sacrifices made today will be worth it tomorrow." As usual, Mama was right. My journey up the career ladder was often bumpy, but remembering those sayings provided hope, calmed anxieties, and nudged me to keep going. As I matured, I interpreted the proverbs as messages of comfort from the ancestors who endured much more than I could ever imagine.

I was born in a household with parents who deprived themselves of things like fancy clothes, respectable shoes, and deserving vacations, even though we lived on an island that boasts world-renowned exotic resort hotels. Saving money was a delusion because every extra dollar went toward schooling and other needs for the three children. My parents believed that for us, education would unlock doors that were never opened to them. Attending school also meant building a brighter future for generations to come. My parents also planted seeds of thriftiness that have grown abundantly and manifested in how I save, invest, and spend. I have learned to stay focused on my goals and avoid instant gratification. Although I am not sure who said that patience is a virtue, I have heard the quote repeatedly, and my experiences validate its truth.

When you sign on to be a teacher, college classes will not fully prepare you for real life in the classroom: inordinate amount of time spent beyond the workday engaging in work-related activities like grading papers, preparing lessons, participating in endless meetings and mandatory professional development activities, or supporting students in extracurricular concert performances or sports. College does not alert teachers how to handle unexpected parent meetings initiated by caregivers in places like the supermarket checkout line, doctor's office, or at off-campus little league events, a quiet dinner out with family, and encroachment on personal time and space.

Neither does college warn potential teachers about legal imposition, in places like Florida, that give the public access to personal information, including previous evaluations and disciplinary records. Therefore, future parents can investigate educators' backgrounds before enrolling children in school or classes.

The nightly news and print media constantly show ills within education. High-stakes testing help create labels like good and bad schools and teachers. The finger-pointing at teachers sometimes leaves us weary and disrespected. Still, it is important to note that neighbors love their schools and their teachers insomuch that our presence is requested on community boards and to lead organizations, be guest speakers for functions, and continue to be a moral compass for society. Teachers carry this burden while preparing young people to lead in the twenty-first century.

I love to read different types of books, especially biographies, because learning about people's struggles and success strategies gives me hope and contributes to my life's road map. The stories teach me survival tips from women who, in addition to taking care of family and career responsibilities, still obtained advanced degrees. I completed a doctorate in education degree in a grueling three-year period because others showed me that it was possible. Over those years, I abandoned a social life, restricted impulsive shopping, piled up student loans, survived on sleep deprivation, and never took a sabbatical from my teaching job. Looking back, the outcome was worth the sacrifice.

Starting with my parents, I learned to trust my instincts and to be visionary. When I began studies for a master's degree in educational leadership, my employer's compensation policy was limited to people in certain leadership positions. Unfortunately, my job category was excluded. Despite many attempts to secure scholarships or grants and with escalating costs for schooling, I was not dissuaded from pursuing my dreams. Obtaining a doctorate degree was a personal goal. I would be the first in my family to take that gigantic step. Convinced that my job outlook and career advancements would increase, I proceed with school, a decision I never regretted.

Humans are creatures of habits. We appreciate our comfort zone and are reluctant to change habits. Teachers are no exceptions. Familiarity with curriculum and grade-level standards, expected outcomes, and effortless planning are contributing factors to decisions teachers make to refrain from transferring to other schools or grade levels. I have an associate who taught first grade in the same classroom for thirty years. A reluctance to make a change could interfere with possibilities for advancements.

I love to learn and welcome opportunities to teach different grade levels or subjects, not intimidated by being the newest person on the block, embarrassed to ask endless questions, or worse, to be vulnerable to embark on a steep learning curve. Whenever a principal asked for volunteers to teach in a different capacity, I would be the first to volunteer. The opportunity to teach at other levels boosted my knowledge of what works in schools and provided information about the skills and knowledge expected of students before they entered or exited my class. However, I did not initially see the total value of my flexibility on my career until I had an interview for my first elementary school assistant principal's position. In the interview, I had to share my knowledge of schoolwide curriculum and appropriate strategies. My confidence and diverse experiences also helped to land me the position of director of elementary education.

Making sacrifices is about facing adversities and pushing through despite the odds. When I was told that I only qualified for a teacher's aide job, I had a choice to settle, give up, or get on track with my dreams. Despite the seen and unseen obstacles, I decided to go back to school. I defied the odds and had no regrets about the countless sacrifices.

The decision to further my education was not just for me. I had sleepless nights, disappointed in myself when my grades were horrible, masked my anxieties and fears, and cried when no one was watching. However, I could not afford a prolonged pity party. I persevered because it was important that my children and fellow educators see value in my journey and learn that they too can achieve despite hardships.

I believe mother, teacher, and role model are synonymous terms. I tried to show that it was remarkable to begin a task and even more fulfilling to bring it to fruition. Teachers have a responsibility to teach coping strategies. Give students opportunities to be heard. Help them identify events or activities that create tensions or outbursts and provide appropriate tools or resources. Engage students in discussions about failure, a natural phenomenon that does not have to be incapacitating. Children also need to see examples of successful people.

Each setback and recovery made me stronger. The lessons learned and opportunities to share the experiences of my journey have been more impactful than certificates and trophies.

Teachers' Corner

1. Describe the most extraordinary personal or professional sacrifice you ever made. How did the event change your life?

2. Who do you think has sacrificed the most for you? How have you or will you repay?

3. How do you juggle your time to be of help to others?

4. Which aspect of your life is a lesson worth sharing with students or coworkers?

5. How will you share the information identified in question 4?

6. If you had to do it all over again, would you still become a teacher, knowing the salary and intrusion on your time and life? If so, why?

7. What keeps you motivated?

8. List the people in your support system.

9. If you do not have advanced degrees, are you planning to go back to school? Why or why not?

10. If you have graduate degrees, what were the motivating factors for pursuing them?

Digging In

1. Write an article for a professional magazine or create the outline for a book, sharing sacrifices you made to achieve your goals.

2. To enjoy financial stability in retirement, meet with a financial planner to develop a realistic savings and budget plan. Once created, monitor your progress and make necessary adjustments. Think long term.

3. Teach students the benefits of delayed gratification using specific examples. One strategy for younger students is to have incentive parties at the end of the week. For older students, waiting until the end of the semester is beneficial. Elaborate celebrations are not necessary; students will respond positively to any acknowledgments.

4. Before holidays like Thanksgiving, Christmas, or Hanukkah, brainstorm with students' ways to bring cheer to others in the community. For example, serve meals at a food pantry, sing to the elderly in neighborhood nursing homes, or perform holiday songs in public spaces like a mall or hospital lobby.

5. Encourage families and friends to join you in adopting a child or a family for the holidays. Once identified, interview the adoptees to get an idea of likes, dislikes, and dreams. Giving to others is a sacrifice worth making.

10

Network

AS MENTIONED, AT THE AGE OF FIVE, I KNEW I WANTED to be a teacher. I would play school in my bedroom with dolls, and on weekends or during long summer breaks, my students were the green shrubs and beautiful flowers surrounding our house, evidence of my mother's green thumb that added calm and beauty to the small wood-framed country house we called home before I was born.

In my mind, I was the best teacher because my students were compliant. I proudly imitated instructional and discipline behaviors of my favorite teachers at the small community elementary school where I grew up and where all my childhood friends attended. I believe my friends would all agree that it was evident I would end up being a teacher.

At school, I was the teacher's pet, always eager to volunteer for classroom tasks and looking forward to getting tiny stubs of discarded chalk as a reward for my hard work. I believe my teachers saw me as a reflection of their younger selves—bright-eyed and eager to teach.

I loved school because I was surrounded by caring and supportive people. School was an extension of my home.

Mama and Daddy, with shoulders rising with pride, often jokingly bragged about my teaching antics. "She is one devoted teacher, but heaven help those children," Daddy would say, referring to the repeated floggings I perpetrated on my students—the beautiful ferns, dieffenbachias, red and yellow hibiscus, birds-of-paradise, and even the morning glory that lifted their red flowers at the crack of sunlight and went back to sleep at sundown. It does not matter how excited I got; I knew not to touch Mama's orchids, which were her pride and joy.

In my rural community, whipping children was a long tradition. However, the practice satisfies only the person inflicting the pain. Unfortunately, the punishment does more to generate fear and show cruelty rather than change juvenile behaviors. For example, my brother got his share of beatings for skipping school; the sting lasted temporarily, and his misbehavior continued. In my early days, all adults literally obeyed Proverbs 13:24: "He that spareth his rod hateth his son: but he that loveth him chaseth him in good season."

Most of all, Mama regularly communicated with teachers not just to check on my academic progress but to look to them to nurture teaching aspirations. I still remember sleepovers at my mentors' homes (it was legal back then), and our lively exchanges about trade books like *Alice's Adventures in Wonderland* (Carroll 1865), *Little Women* (Alcott 1881), *Great Expectations* (Dickens 1996), the unforgettable *Hardy Boys Adventure* (Dixon 2016), and the Nancy Drew Mystery series (Keene 1930). My support system affected my life in countless ways, including the notion that mentoring and networking will positively change someone's life. I took that to heart, and today I serve as a mentor to people of all ages.

Another of Mama's favorite sayings was "Show me your friends and I will tell you who you are." Therefore, I learned early to surround myself with people who shared similar interests and enthusiasm for life and who genuinely cared for my wellbeing. As a classroom instructor, I participated in several school-based committees, even though I overextended myself at times. As a participating member, I eagerly shared classroom activities and best practices gleaned from research. In turn, I gained valuable information to help my students while advancing my career opportunities. I learned about school operations, improved communication and leadership skills, and interacted with influential people. The experiences prepared me for future instructional and administrative positions.

Throughout graduate school, I sought help from colleagues who became members of my critical support system. When I needed student participation for practicum activities, finding classrooms was not difficult. The team unselfishly shared their students and thoughtfully offered a helping hand throughout my studies.

People in our circles should keep us accountable, whether it is our mothers with their brutal honesty, supervisors through timely feedback after classroom observations and evaluation, and constructive criticism from peers. A supervisor once gave me an average rating on an end-of-year evaluation. I thought I deserved above average. I was hurt and disappointed. While I did not agree with the explanation that "the low score was intended to push me to realize my potential," from that day on, I worked diligently to improve identified weak areas with a determination to never receive such poor marks in the future. Today that supervisor remains a mentor who offers complimentary remarks and is excited about my pursuits.

My network also consists of my husband and adult children. It is difficult to accept criticisms from immediate family members because of the possibilities for inflamed passions. However, I know my compassionate family unit will rise above differences to help as needed.

Completing graduate school required enormous resilience, juggling many and changing responsibilities of parenting, working two jobs, volunteering at various community events, and serving on numerous committees. Maintaining a healthy school life balance was difficult. One helpful strategy was to post my school and work schedules on the refrigerator door at home. The visual served as a motivator for me and gave my family an opportunity to organize activities around my schedule so that I could participate, and above all, my children witnessed the necessity for hard work and dedication to achieve goals. The dominant message conveyed was that we were all in the ebb and flow together and my achievements meant our accomplishments.

Grown-ups realize the importance of a supportive network, yet it is a skill to be mastered. Make a conscious decision to reach out as often as possible to at least one person in your area of interest—for example, a school principal if there is a plan to become an administrator. Join reputable social media groups and platforms. Connect with influential people within the profession, like area supervisors and school superintendents. Work on communication skills. Volunteer to conduct workshops with your peers or within the community. Learn to listen. Be sincere.

Young people should be taught know how to find and leverage a compassionate and enthusiastic team. First help them to identify positive behaviors in friends or people seen on television. When I was a classroom teacher, I also taught essential character traits like respect, responsibility, courage, and honesty. By providing specific examples, I hoped that students would be drawn to others with similar characteristics.

When I was a school principal, I asked teachers to volunteer to be mentors to students who were facing academic and behavioral challenges. Volunteers would reach out to students in simple ways, visiting mentees' classrooms, offering a safe time-out space in mentors' classroom when necessary, listening, giving thumbs-up or pats on the back for a positive start of the school day, or checking on progress throughout the day and monitoring and providing support for school success. The mentorship program had a tremendous positive impact on student achievement, attitude toward school and learning and improved classroom and school tone. Importantly, students understood that school is more than just teaching content knowledge.

Hard work is not always acknowledged, but I am proof that it is noticed, especially by persons looking for talent. While I was serving on committees within and beyond the school doors, some individuals in leading positions in the school district and within the community at large were learning about me and observing my progress, work ethic, and effectiveness. By the time I was ready to advance into the leadership realm, my name elicited positive testimonials.

Today, as an education consultant, I look back and realize that I was unknowingly creating a brand, a marketing strategy. In my role as a college professor, I give an assignment that requires students to conduct informal interviews with someone currently practicing or retired from a career in which there is interest. The task has a multidimensional reason. First, it serves to improve research, communication, and interviewing skills. Second, it expands students' knowledge about a possible job while developing or expanding a professional network.

When I was in elementary school, field trips were fun. Etched in my memory is the picture of children and chaperones rocking from side to side and bouncing up and down on the back of a truck, the usual mode of transportation for educational trips on near or far journeys. The lorry had a wooden frame with vertical pieces of wood creating the body and held securely to the base of the truck. Our seat was several flat, sturdy planks of wood stretching horizontally along the width of the truck and held in place between the spaces of the vertical pieces. Seat belts were not part of the design.

Safety was not a concern, as we happily belted out familiar cultural and sacred songs along the winding potholed country roads. Without prompting, individuals took turns starting songs. Sometimes each row sang a verse while the other occupants acted as backup singers joining in with the chorus. More than four decades later the song "The More We Get Together", rekindles pleasant memories of my childhood with forever friends and mentors. The words to this song affirmed that we need each other, and we are stronger together.

Teachers' Corner

1. List the people who make up your support system. Identify the nature and value of each relationship.

2. Suppose you have been asked to give a speech to graduating high school seniors on the topic of networking. What would you say? Please list your talking points.

3. Do you market yourself and your skills? If so, how?

4. Other than teaching, how are you involved in your school or community?

5. List at least five strategies you will use to begin a networking campaign. How will you hold yourself accountable?

6. What is your communication style? How is your approach helping or hurting your abilities and opportunities to network?

7. What steps can you take to help others be the best of themselves and flourish?

8. Describe people you know who are excellent at networking. What behaviors do they exhibit?

9. How are you an active listener?

10. Describe an event or activity in which you took the initiative to plan and lead. What were the goals, and how did you evaluate the outcomes?

Digging In

1. Invite at least five of your closest friends to lunch or afternoon tea. Share your goals—for example, a desire to go back to school. You may solicit support for proofreading papers, for babysitting, or for carpooling for school drop-off or picking up.

2. Join a gym. Support from a health-conscious community will provide motivation, opportunities to network, and expand your knowledge about health and wellness.

3. Cooperative learning groups help students become responsible members of a community. Have students form groups by choosing team members. Sometimes you may have to intervene to ensure that all students are included in the process. Students should move within groups to experience the benefits of working with people from diverse backgrounds and with different points of view.

4. Start writing a professional blog about a topic of which you are passionate. Be appropriate, consistent, and authentic with postings.

5. Teach students how to be active listeners. For example, model how to give a speaker undivided attention. Inform students that after a presentation, follow-up questions or activities will be conducted. Suggest body languages that convey attentive listening.

11

Appreciate and Ignore Naysayers

WOVEN IN STEPS UP THE SUCCESS LADDER IS A WILLINGness to take risks. I have met people who invested every dime they own to a venture in which they believe. Most endured growing pains and stuck with their passion, which eventually produced positive results. On the other hand, some people prefer stability and will not hesitate to express concerns or disdain for daredevils. Still others will coax and cajole you away from your dreams. I call discouragers "naysayers," and they have the power to positively and negatively affect one's career.

One of the most significant professional risks I took was to answer the call to lead one of the lowest-performing schools in my district. A supervisor who always supported my aspirations was skeptical, concerned, and discouraged about the pending transfer. I had confidence and trust in my abilities to turn the school around, so I persevered. I developed a strategic plan and doggedly monitored implementation. We successfully turned the school around. Had I listened to my supervisor, I would not have experienced a significant life-changing event, one that tested my talents and skills, put me in the spotlight, and importantly crushed stereotypes of teaching and learning in urban settings.

In my desperation to revive my teaching career after moving to the United States of America, I took a bold step to begin the process. Upon hearing that the only position for which I qualified was a teacher's aide, the disappointment and hopelessness were overwhelming. Before moving to the United States, I was enjoying a successful stable teaching career, devoting my life to be the best instructor any child could have. After receiving the hopeless news and temporarily sinking into disbelief, thinking my dreams and hopes had dashed, I pulled myself together and registered in a teacher education program. Exactly two years later, I was the recipient of a Bachelor of Science degree in elementary education, and ten years later, I added another title, Doctor of Education. I shudder to think what my life would be if I ignored the encouraging voice from within pushing me to take the jump. The disadvantages were stacked against me: challenges to carve out extra time to study after working two jobs, finding monies to cover school expenses, raising a young family, and having only one car, with members of the family going in different directions.

I learned several lessons from the dramatic school turnaround project. Throughout the yearlong school reform process, the faculty and I worked hard to procure the coveted "A" prize. As student data improved, so did faith in the reform plan's strategies. The team galvanized around its mission with unrelenting fervor, a more unified energy never seen in the school. The closer we got to test day, confidence from staff, students, and parents soared. Unfortunately, several factions in the school district categorized me as delusional because history showed that schools with such complexities would have a difficult time overcoming insurmountable challenges to rise to the top of the grading scale within one school year. I ignored the chatter, aware that there will always be someone to plant seeds of doubt or discourage dreams.

A deep sense of satisfaction emanates from proving nonbelievers wrong. The drastic school transformation shocked the system. We proved that a knowledgeable and dedicated school team, partners with parents and the community could muffle naysayers.

I have established that pessimists can be dream busters. Does that mean we should banish them from our lives? It may not be possible if the perpetrator is a member of the faculty or a parent; therefore, generating alternative strategies may be the only choice. When I was a third-grade teacher, a sensitive issue surfaced when a parent verbalized doubts in my abilities to teach her child because of my foreign background and accent. The dilemma was that the child could not be moved to another class, for I was the only teacher of reading and language arts for gifted students at that grade level. To make matters worse, no other vacant teaching positions existed within the area, so transferring me was not an option. The obvious solution was for teacher and student continue to work together, at least through the end of the school year.

For the students' sake, I jumped into action, deciding that a way to alleviate fears and quell ignorance was to work more earnestly at implementing innovative and successful instructional strategies. My goal was to show that regardless of my heritage and accent, I was a competent professional who was determined to help each child succeed. The competitor in me was determined to prove a point and silently gloated in anticipation of hearing the mother acknowledge that her baseless assessment was inaccurate. Not only did the words I was expecting come, but she requested a younger sibling to enroll in my class for the following school year.

Life is a progression of setting and achieving goals. When folks around us are genuinely happy, eagerly celebrating and embracing our accomplishments, we feel fulfilled. Without fail, though, a cynic or skeptic is always lurking around, ready to steal joy. The disguise may be jealousy masked as concerns. Despite the reasons, offensive remarks tend to remain in the head of the receiver and can have somber effects.

I have been discouraged from taking additional certification courses because the stress of taking classes would be overwhelming and detrimental to my health. Stress and anxiety are both counterproductive and manageable behaviors. I remained cognizant of the bearer of the concern, taking heed but continuing to keep studying and remaining devoted to my goals. When the behavior of others begins to affect our souls and attitudes negatively, it may be time to rethink and reevaluate such relationships.

I once had a friend who seemed to drain all my energy and my self-esteem whenever we met or exchanged conversations. I realized that I felt worse rather than uplifted after each interaction, which left me rehashing the unfavorable discussions. Eventually, I decided to end the relationship.

We cannot always point fingers at others. Too often the negative voices we hear coming from our heads stem primarily from lack of confidence and fear of the unknown. How do we turn off the annoying voices that have the potential to do considerable emotional damage? First recommit to the vision, mission, and goals.

Create a vision board as a visual and daily reminder. Acknowledge and celebrate successes, small and large. Trust your abilities, instincts, and values. Do not dismiss the power of intuition. Be aware of your self-worth, which comprises thoughts, feelings, and actions.

Be familiar with the people in your sphere of influence. Avoid people who appear to have control or power over you. Exercise self-love, the most significant love of all. Shower yourself with the kind of empathy and affection you readily give to others. Face your fears and acknowledge that you are not your fear, which is a temporary phenomenon. Remind yourself that like fear, failure is a momentary setback usually experienced on the path to success.

After working with various age groups from diverse backgrounds in numerous educational settings, I have learned a great deal from young people. Ignoring negative comments is a more difficult task for children and adolescents, for they tend to be easily influenced by social media as well as words and actions of people around them. So how do adults help youths combat the effects of unpleasant language or hostile energy? Surround them with positive role models. Promote and facilitate ways to develop resilience and coping skills. Teach problem-solving and critical thinking skills. Show young people how to accept and work through failures. Demonstrate and nurture positivity. Celebrate real successes and avoid building false hope.

I have met and prevailed over doubters in every phase and age of my life. Some people's actions and words were more painful than others were and unfortunately lingered in my psyche longer than necessary. However, over the years, I have developed survival strategies for personal and professional success. I learned not to take things too personally. I have worked vigorously to dismiss negative thoughts, to ignore dubious points of view that hijack joy. Ending relationships is not a pleasant or enjoyable undertaking, but it is occasionally unavoidable. Decide on a tolerance level and do not give permission to anyone to deprive you of success.

Teachers' Corner

1. Who are the naysayers in your life? How do you know? How do you handle them?

2. List at least five ways in which you limit your potential.

3. Describe the vision for your life.

4. Describe the most courageous thing you ever did. What were the circumstances? How did the action influence your life?

5. Have you ever been told you cannot or should not do something? If so, how did you react?

6. Have you ever met a student who reminded you of yourself? If so, how did you work with the student?

7. When you look backward in your professional life, what and who do you see? Please explain.

8. Describe and define two significant characteristics of the people you most admire. What do you have in common with those people?

9. How can you determine the difference between a pessimist and a person who is looking out for your best interests?

10. Do you believe that if you spend too much time with naysayers, you will eventually become like them? Please explain.

Digging In

1. Practice polite ways of saying no to unsolicited advice. Find ways to promote systematically quality relationships in your work setting.

2. Create a committee geared toward turning around pessimistic behaviors.

3. Invite a naysayer to lunch and politely express your frustrations. What outcome would you expect from the meeting? Sometimes by developing a deeper understanding of each other, more common ground is established. It may be necessary to set ground rules for meetings.

4. Naysayers tend to cluster around each other, especially in faculty meetings or in the faculty room, therefore affecting the school's climate. To combat the constant undermining, it may be necessary to elicit the help of an expert. Getting objective information is always beneficial.

5. Give students opportunities to participate in debates about current, cultural, or historical events. Younger students may discuss character similarities and differences in a story being read by the class.

12

Believe

ON MY FIRST DAY AS PRINCIPAL OF PINE GROVE Elementary School, I took several boxes of the book *The Little Engine That Could* (Piper 1976), a copy for every child. Within the first hour, all the students had either read the book by themselves, with the help of a teacher, or as a read aloud by the teacher, with every class then engaged in discussion about the meaning of the book.

I wanted students to believe that within them is power to inspire success. The standardized test data showed bleakness with a downward trend. Internalizing the possibility and creating a winning path was not always easy for students, parents, teachers, or the community. However, over time, academic achievement showed promise and inappropriate behaviors declined. Attendance improved, students took more responsibility for their own learning, and teachers proudly mastered efficacy. The implementation of a comprehensive schoolwide approach transformed the school, but without a doubt, it helped students believe in their own possibilities, which was critical in the process.

As discussed in chapter 7, setting goals help us to live with a purpose. Achieving goals reinforces a can-do attitude. By setting daily class goals, I also help students understand that each day presents another opportunity to learn, grow, and achieve.

Watch the language you use to describe yourself. I had a student who would constantly call himself stupid. He internalized that belief, so his confidence mirrored what he thought about himself. He rarely took risks and needed validation from others. On the contrast, students with a keen sense of self are mostly high-spirited and have an eagerness to learn.

My parents planted a seed of greatness within me. Their actions, not necessarily words, showed me that I could achieve. With limited education, they developed vocational and entrepreneurial skills that allowed them to educate three children, provide a home and financial support to many others, and offer apprenticeship opportunities to countless others. Alexander and Gwendolyn Scott also demonstrated that strength of self also comes from being of service to others. They were community leaders in their own rights, ensuring kids and the needy in the community were protected. People knew that there was always an extra plate at our dinner table, and especially at Christmastime, anyone was welcome to dine with us.

Help students understand that failure is a natural phenomenon. Teachers can show students that everyone makes mistakes, even the teacher. As much as possible, I give students opportunities to correct mistakes.

Mental doubts are a confidence killer. Encourage students to participate in mentorship programs. Teach strategies on how to forgive self. Have students send positive notes to each other. Help students understand that friendships can be fickle so there is no need to fall apart when a friendship ends.

Knowledge is power, which also translates to self-confidence. I obtained graduate degrees because I believed I could. Attaining advanced degrees opened unimaginable career doors for me. In addition, to be acknowledged and respected for my research and given platforms to speak on various topics certainly elevated my self-esteem. A child-centered classroom provides rich learning opportunities that encourage critical thinking and reasoning. A natural outgrowth is promoting love of learning. I invite guest speakers to talk about topics like careers, health and wellness, and community service projects.

Chapter 8 encourages continuous education. In addition to the added benefits like increased pay, stimulating intellectual growth, and improving teaching and learning, expanded knowledge will help teachers approach their jobs more confidently.

Teachers should also teach about learning styles and multiple intelligences. It is critical to help students understand the different ways they receive and process information and the many innate ways to demonstrate smartness. Giving students choices on assignments builds trust, develops independence, and provides practice in knowing more about themselves and how they should study.

NO ONE ESCAPES DIFFICULT TIMES; THE DIFFERENCE LIES in the way we rise to face them. Some people get overwhelmed and freeze, unable to find solutions. Some people tap into resources for help. Then there are those who see problems like a puzzle to be solved and once done move on. The latter group has a healthy relationship with problem-solving. Their self-belief gives power over challenges. Similarly, teachers handle discipline problems differently.

Some teachers repeatedly call the office for help. Others seek help from coworkers. Still others never seem to have issues in their classrooms.

Believing that I could help, influence, and significantly affect someone's life is one of the miracles of my life. In the early years, I did not have a measure of my impact. Now, with decades of teaching behind me and scores of students and teachers later, I feel confident that I am living up to the expectations that I envisioned.

Believing in me has been an ongoing learning experience and driving force that involved commitment and patience. I learned to rise each morning knowing that each day brings new opportunities to learn something new or to build on what I previously started. I am not an anomaly. We all can succeed. We must believe.

Teachers' Corner

1. Are you living the life of which you dreamed? How or why not?

2. Keep a notepad close and record each time in a day that you think of or utter the words "I can't."

3. List at least five ways you demonstrate that you trust and love yourself.

4. Identify your greatest self-doubt. What actions are you taking to relieve yourself of its potentially debilitating impact?

5. What is your most significant career achievement? How did it happen?

6. List at least five people in your circle who believe, support, and share your goals and aspirations.

7. How do you shut down the negative voices in your head?

8. List five strategies that you use to help your students believe in themselves.

9. What thoughts keep you up at night?

10. List at least ten words that describe you.

Digging In

Upon waking every morning, do the following routine before getting out of bed:

1. Tell yourself something about you or about what you are doing that makes you proud.

2. Set a realistic goal, aligned with your mission, to be accomplished that day.

3. Find a way to be of service to someone in need, such as visiting a person who is shut in, calling someone you have not spoken to in a while, or making a delivery for Meals on Wheels.

4. At the end of the day, assess if you reached the day's goal.

5. Make time to list personal and professional accomplishments. Probably you baked a pie for the first time or challenged your fears of dancing in public. If returning to college is on your mind, today is the day to start the process.

6. The world is not lacking causes in need of volunteers. Locate an agency that supports a conviction you have. While helping others, you may discover skills you never thought you had.

7. At the end of each day, pause to reflect on events and how you maneuvered yourself. Take credit and responsibility. Probably you had to tolerate the extreme behaviors of a child in crisis or you counted to ten instead of saying something you may later regret.

8. Believe that the sky and beyond is your limit. Work each day to align your behaviors and thoughts with your goals. Push yourself to walk or run an extra mile. Conduct research on how to achieve a goal of participating in a study abroad program or to teach in an international program.

13

Manage Details

GAUDI'S UNFINISHED SAGRADA FAMILIA BASILICA IN Barcelona, Spain, is among the most significant and captivating masterpieces I have seen. I am still in awe of the intricate details that showed the artist's sophisticated thinking and artistry. Despite his passing, leaving an unfinished structure, Mr. Gaudi's fastidiousness has allowed artists to continue the work. Details do matter.

Kudos to the inventor of Post-it Notes. I have stuck notes reminders everywhere: on the refrigerator door, on the personal computer and laptop, and on the bathroom mirror. I am detailed oriented and believe that paying attention to details is the difference between something being ordinary and extraordinary.

Likewise, when I am getting ready for grocery shopping, I create either a paper or electronic list, which saves time. Saving time on one task allows for more time doing something else, like relaxing.

When I was a classroom teacher, I wrote very detailed lesson plans that included measurable objectives with outcomes, procedures for teacher and students, resource materials, extension activities, activities for special learners, guest speakers (if any), and approximate length and time for questions and answers and formative assessment. Creating detailed plans saves time on preparation, allowing more time for instruction and student practice.

In all leadership roles, I held regularly scheduled meetings. All faculty meetings were held monthly and team/curriculum meetings weekly. Each meeting was announced, and an agenda developed. Notifications help all stakeholders with personal planning. Agendas serve several purposes that include documenting topics and note-taking, keeping the audience focused and useful for follow-up. Attachments were included with the agenda. I kept a binder with all relevant documents. I have had occasions when my notes were subpoenaed, or I have had to refer to the documentations in meetings with teachers. Keeping detailed notes and records is essential.

Each night before going to bed, I check my calendar for the next day. This habit prepares me for the day ahead. I may have to prepare PowerPoint presentations, send out reminders to attendees of meetings, check previous notes if a follow-up meeting is scheduled, or collect information from others. When planning the calendar, it is important to allow enough time for and between meetings. Sometimes meetings last longer than planned, causing you to be late for the next. Whenever possible, notify respective parties. Try not to overbook yourself.

Goal setting cannot be overemphasized. Developing both long-term and short-term goals with specific and realistic expectations is critical to managing details. During implementation of the winning reform model that I created and implemented, executing the plan as designed required strategic coordination with all stakeholders and time to monitor the process. Teachers were required to adhere to class schedules, uninterrupted instruction and curriculum objectives, submit lesson plans as scheduled, keep detailed records of student progress, develop and administer formative and summative evaluations as planned, attend meetings, hold data chats with students, and organize parent-teacher conferences.

An important component of the reform model was realigning the school's budget to support the initiative, like purchasing resource materials, hiring consultants, paying for relevant extracurricular activities, and most importantly, meeting stipend obligations for teachers. At the same time, monies had to be allocated for regular school operation. Naturally, the budget had to be precise.

Planning for job responsibilities was critical; however, just as important was ensuring that I spent quality time with family and friends. Calendar development included time for my kids' school events, like dance recitals, track-and-field events, football games and parent meetings. At the beginning of each week, my husband and I coordinated schedules, a practice that contributed to a less hectic family life.

An effective manager of time schedules time for both work and play. I love to travel, so at the beginning of each year, my family coordinates all schedules to carve out time for vacation. Taking time from work allows the body to relax and improves creativity because there is time for thinking. Therefore, everyone benefits from vacations.

One of the most successful activities for a homeschool connection is the use of calendar books. Using school-based funds, I purchased a calendar book for each student in the elementary school. Kindergarten through fifth grade students wrote daily homework assignments or dates for school activities. Teachers wrote notes to parents, who had an option to respond. Parents could also initiate communication to the teacher. The calendar books did not replace face-to-face conferences but were helpful in building trust and kept everyone informed.

Big issues tend to consume significant time and energy. I believe that too much focus on big stuff detracts from small details and could result in a loss of focus. I attribute my achievements to paying keen attention to details, being a stickler for following protocol, and being organized and committed to my goals, dedication to the profession I love dearly, and out of a sense of duty to my parents and ancestors.

Teachers' Corner

1. What is your "big picture"? How are you getting to it?

2. Describe your project management process.

3. Why do details matter?

4. Describe a method you use to set and keep goals.

5. What does the idiom "The devil is in the details" mean to you?

6. Suppose you have been asked to give a speech on how to manage details. Please write ten tips you will provide.

7. Explain the little things you do to contribute to your success as an educator.

8. Identify at least five small things that could transform your school environment.

9. How do established routines help your class or school? Please provide examples.

10. Write a letter to your younger self. Explain the importance of focusing on small details.

Digging In

1. When planning lessons, focus on small details like listing and gathering all the materials and equipment ahead of teaching and approximate the time needed for each activity. Additionally, include activities to meet learning and personality styles and assist special needs students.

2. Be cognizant of how you spend. Investigate a tool that will help you keep track of where your money goes. Be honest with your recording and adjust accordingly.

3. Organize a committee to plan activities centered on fun faculty activities.

4. Create a list of small details that could improve the school's operation.

5. Create a team to organize an event with a specific purpose.

14

Give

I AM HAPPIEST WHEN SERVING, GIVING TO OTHERS, AND seeing that my efforts make a difference in someone's life. I know that generosity helps to define one's purpose, positively influences overall health, and contributes to peace of mind. I also know teachers who support my belief.

It is no secret that some of the most charitable persons are the teachers who spend millions of dollars from already meager earnings to purchase classroom supplies or to make financial contributions to students, parents, and local charities. Some teachers give to the detriment of their pocketbooks. Yet despite personal sacrifices and job-related stressors, most teachers will quickly admit that quitting for a more lucrative job is out of the question. They favor making a difference in the lives of others and improving communities over monetary rewards.

Throughout my life, I have shown appreciation for exemplary teachers who made a significant impact on my life. I will be forever grateful for the commitment of folks like Ms. Mack, my infant school teacher, and Ms. Haughton, my elementary school teacher and principal. Both women took time to guide me as a young child, and in Ms. Haughton's case, she did all she could to bolster my career, which began at the elementary school I attended. I could not have scripted the events of my illustrious career and will forever salute the numerous heroes and heroines for the part they played.

Over the years, I have encountered educators who remind me of ones long ago, who set me on the path to success. The constancy of their extra efforts and personal interest in my future defined my life. Many years have passed since my remarkable childhood educational experiences, but in various administrative and leadership roles, I met and worked alongside teachers who embodied similar behaviors: giving and loving unconditionally, never giving up on a child, continually researching alternative ways to reach and teach, and taking responsibility for the academic outcomes of children in their charge.

I believe special needs educators should proudly wear a crown. First, deciding to undertake a course of study that focuses on meeting the needs of exceptional learners is commendable. Second, special education teachers should be applauded for exhibiting undeniable patience, demonstrating outstanding flexibility, showing appreciation and acknowledgment for small and large strides students make, and staying positive, no matter the complexities. Third, brave teachers are repeatedly confronted with student behaviors that are not taught in teacher preparation courses and cannot be quantified on an instructor's evaluation instrument or be validated in a paycheck. Yet, the unconditional love and care given to some of the school's most vulnerable students are priceless.

I honor Carmen Bowman; whose patience and knowledge are the best. Tamar Spence incorporated humor into her pedagogy. It made all the difference in the tone and climate of the classroom and student achievement.

Amoi Spence was a kindergarten teacher who took great pride to ensure that all her students were fluent readers by the end of the school year. She believed every child, despite the readiness skills, could meet reading expectations. She accelerated and remediated as needed before, during, and after school. Her primary complaint was not having enough time in a day to do more for her students; she affectionally called her babies. Without checking data, Amoi could articulate the reading level of each child. She never threw out discontinued materials, for those discarded items, may be the resource that helps a child succeed. I dubbed her "Master Kindergarten Teacher."

Sharon James-Burton, Dellis Brown Beal, Sharon Robinson and Lorna Smith epitomized excellence for both themselves and students. These women went beyond the typical duties to find innovative and creative strategies to motivate and engage students, resulting in high levels of student performance accompanied by immense pride. These dedicated teachers needed more time because the regular school hours were not enough to get the job done, so they worked beyond hours almost every day.

Every school has students with chronic absences or tardiness. At our school, Pamela Camel made it her mission to break the lateness cycle. Many of the truants did not have a healthy relationship with school. As often as possible, Dr. Camel transported students who were not excited about giving up home for school and, with the help of mentors, changed anti-school behaviors. It was not unusual for Pamela to purchase shoes and clothing items for needy students. Her job was her mission.

Gregory Kirkwood grew up in the community in which he taught. He knew the parents and sometimes grandparents of pupils in the school. Greg treated students and parents like family. He attended community events and initiated activities that brought the school and its community together, resulting in improved mutual trust and respect. Such skills are not taught in teachers' training programs but are developed and enhanced through a desire to give more than is required.

Sandra Moreau Oliver made the challenging job of coordinating the English for Speakers of Other Languages (ESOL) program look easy. She took the job personally, as if she had given birth to every child.

Shanda Davis's creativity kept students engaged and returning every day for more. Jeannie Langford and Candy Waring were a tag team who exemplified the meaning of collaboration. Their students were the real victors in the situation.

Aside from improved student achievement, moments that gave me joy included catering meals for teachers or treating outstanding students to lunch. After each event, I felt rewarded and at peace. My actions contributed to improved teacher and student morale, and I know my health also benefited.

One year I asked each grade level to adopt a family for the holidays. We got clothes and shoes for each person in the household, toys for each child, and granted food requests. Grade levels engaged parents and the community in the process. On the last day for collecting items, I was stunned with the energy and generosity. We had to get trucks to haul donations. The activity brought our school community together in an incredible manner. Above all, we showed students the importance and value of giving.

Giving is contagious. When others witness your generosity, it is likely that they will want to give as well. Giving creates social bonds, as evidenced by the Caribbean Educators Association (C.A.R.E) Inc., a nonprofit organization that provides scholarships to graduating high school seniors. In 2005, along with like-minded friends, I founded C.A.R.E simply to give back. I did so because countless persons advocated, provided direct assistance, or offered a safe place for me to land. Not only did I feel it was my responsibility to give back, but the feeling I get from reaching out to total strangers has been life changing.

I approach the beginning of each fiscal year with a fervent desire to raise more funds than the previous year to increase the number of scholarships awarded. I have developed marketing skills that I never knew I possessed, becoming an event planner who hosts numerous events to raise funds for scholarships. I have advanced leadership, networking, and communication skills through ongoing social engagements.

Kindness is a choice and a universal language with a rippling effect. Students and parents appreciate and admire teachers who show mindfulness and empathy. In my role as assistant superintendent with responsibilities for alternative schools and related programs, I regularly went to the Palm Beach County Juvenile Correction facilities to visit incarcerated youth, not because I had to but from a desire to maintain hope for children in crisis. Parents expressed gratitude for my visits, but the smiles attempting to hide confusion and fright are etched in my memory. After each visit to the jail, I left with a sense of gratitude for a job that allowed me to give back in such an unusual way.

When teachers model kindness and caring, students typically work hard to please, often resulting in improved academics and social behaviors. Classrooms become calmer, happier, and more caring.

Giving to students does not have to be an extravagant or elaborate event. Sometimes giving small things matters in significant ways. I would travel to classrooms with a pocketful of goodies like pencils, erasers, and stickers, with arms ready to give hugs. I loved the thrill students got when I drew a smiley face on a paper. Students walked a little taller and faces shone brighter with the mention of their names on the school's public address system. The display of public praise not only warms the heart of receivers but also has a similar effect on all listeners.

My parents taught me that my life would always have meaning if I gave unconditionally to others. Life experiences have taught me that giving is a habit that once started cannot be stopped and that giving is not about the giver but without a doubt for the persons on the receiving end. We are placed on this earth to be of service to each other.

Teachers' Corner

1. Name something you recently gave to someone. To whom did you give? How did you feel?

2. Discuss the phrase "Giving is getting."

3. Identify at least five philanthropists you know or of whom you have heard. Describe their personalities or characteristics.

4. What is the most delightful gift you ever received? Please explain its significance.

5. How do you encourage students to give to others?

6. Name a charity you support and explain why.

7. How are gratitude and giving similar or different?

8. Finish this sentence: Generosity is _____.

9. If you won a lot of money, how would you spend it? Please explain the reason.

10. What does give of yourself mean to you?

Digging In

1. Set up a gratitude jar in your classroom or home. Deposit coins when you feel grateful. At the end of a specified period, cash in the change and purchase something for somebody.

2. Volunteer to be a mentor to a child not currently in your class.

3. Try regifting some of the gifts you receive.

4. Contribute to your local food bank.

5. Slow down to offer a smile or word of encouragement to someone.

15

Watch the Money

TEACHERS POSITIVELY INFLUENCE SOCIETY, CHANGE and/or add value to people's lives, instill hope for a brighter future, impact generations, build eternal bridges, and are contributors to the economy. Teachers are also surrogate parents, career coaches, mentors, and counselors. Despite hard work, predominance, and respectability in communities, teachers are grossly underpaid and, in many instances, must work several years climbing the slow-rising salary scale before earning a reasonable living wage.

Every teacher I meet would like to retire early with enough funds to make the nonworking years comfortable and less stressful. Individuals who manage to retire with a significant nest egg spent working years exercising some type of money management strategies. We all have different needs, expenses, and spending habits, yet one commonality is setting financial goals on a teacher's salary, especially for a family with young children or teenagers getting ready for college.

I know the life of a teacher struggling to make ends meet between paychecks. When my husband and I first arrived in the United States, we each brought two suitcases crammed full of clothes and a few pairs of shoes. A bright red leather bag held our prized collection of Jim Reeves's long-playing record albums and several reggae hits. The bag was heavy, and at the time, lugging it appeared frivolous considering we had no record player. However, that indulgence turned out to be a significant source of entertainment during dreary winter days in Louisiana and opportunities to reminisce on a happy-go-lucky life of former times. We boarded the plane with two young children who were somewhat scared to be taking their first airplane ride. My thoughts raced back and forth between lofty ideas of purchasing beautiful furniture and household items for the first apartment in the States and images of going shopping for fancy clothes advertised on television. Our hopes and dreams were bigger than the vast country we were about to call home.

Before long, reality took control. Challenges of migration administered harsh punches. Low-paying hourly jobs replaced professional jobs we once enjoyed. Dreams of a comfortable life vanished into the clouds and were replaced with living from paycheck to paycheck, prioritizing and purchasing just to satisfy basic needs. I came face-to-face with a kind of poverty never experienced.

We needed a survival plan. My husband and I designed and implemented a plan. We packed our lunches to avoid eating out, which can be very costly. Our children ate lunch from the school's cafeteria. We no longer assumed that correct change was returned when paying with cash, so we recounted the money. Similarly, we reviewed cash register receipts for any possible errors. I mastered bargain shopping, appreciating the value of couponing.

To get a grip on spending, we started tracking expenses like food, rent, utilities, transportation, and everyday household items. We abandoned socializing and entertainment. The kids made up games and played in the small apartment. My husband and I decided that only the kids could get sick. Despite the tightening of our belt, income was still insufficient, so I got a second job.

Working one job with a young family and trying to adjust to a new life was challenging. Then adding college full time created a new meaning to the word *tired*. However, I clung to the positive aspect that serves me well. Through the process, I learned resilience, determination, and self-empowerment. Habits die hard; I still work two jobs for fear of a return to gripping gut-wrenching fear that results from having too little and barely surviving.

The food bill is amongst the highest expenses in a budget, especially with kids in the household. Therefore, planning a food budget is essential. Plan meals ahead, shopping only for ingredients on the menu lists, which curbs overspending. Cooking large portions and saving leftovers for later not only makes money sense but also saves time spent in the kitchen. Neighborhood grocery stores regularly promote buy-one-get-one deals that provide opportunities to stock up on frequently used items. Buying bulk items in box stores saves money but be mindful of expiration dates. Also be cognizant of unit prices, as buying large quantities is not always worth the saving if the amount is more than what the family needs. When fruits and vegetables are in season, prices will be lower.

The entire family must be involved in monitoring and adjusting consumption of electricity and water. In addition to deriving short-term financial savings, family members who commit to using less power and water are doing their part to save Mother Earth.

Think of paid sick leave as money in the bank, withdrawing funds only when necessary. Use the benefits of sick time leave when there is a real need. You never know when critical illness will strike, requiring extra time away from work. When my son got extremely ill, I had excessive absences. Luckily, I could be with him for the duration. I tapped into my sick leave reserve without losing any wages. Many employment benefit packages include a leave-balance payout at retirement. That's like money is the bank.

Having savings like a 401(k) deducted from earnings and matched by employers provides opportunities for hidden savings. It may be difficult to survive on a smaller paycheck; however, a worthy payday at retirement will be helpful. Additionally, enrolling in automatic payroll deposits minimizes the risk of overspending. Save specifically for vacations, emergency situations like car repairs, to replace appliances, and illnesses, which avoids stress and extravagance. When savings and checking accounts are at separate banks, temptation to spend from the savings is drastically reduced.

Encourage and involve children at home to make customized games that will not only save money but also reinforce critical and creative thinking skills. One of my grandchildren's favorite forms of entertainment is to pretend to play and sing in a band by using paper fans as a guitar and paper cups as microphones. The family enjoys the hilarious performances and spending time together.

Children in school should be taught financial literacy. As a teacher, I worked with my principal to collaborate with a local bank to have banking days at school. With parents' permission, children signed up for bank accounts and deposited small amounts of cash they earned from doing chores at home. Excitement and feelings of accomplishment swelled with a rising account balance. The bankers also provided lectures on money management. My youngest son received his first bank account through this program and paid for his end-of-year field trip at ten years old.

Consult accountants and tax preparers for possible savings through federal and state governments. Another tax benefit is credit given to educators who buy supplies and equipment for classroom use. Be sure to keep all receipts when purchasing items for school.

Take advantage of free activities in local communities. My two-year-old granddaughter enjoys going to the neighborhood library for story hour. No cost is involved in the activity. Saving is not the only benefit from participating in the library activity. Engaging young children in stories and books outside of school helps reinforce the importance of reading.

Whether one finds himself on the lowest rung or having topped out of the pay scale ladder, the key to financial independence is creating and maintaining a realistic budget to which all involved are committed. By itself, money may not guarantee happiness, but having enough evokes a sense of security and independence, having resources to help others, and importantly fulfills your life's dreams.

Teachers' Corner

1. Do you have an itemized budget? If so, please describe your budget.

2. Do you have a saving style? If you do, please explain.

3. Are you an impulsive buyer? What can you do to curtail the habit?

4. Do you have money in an interest-bearing bank account? If so, are you satisfied with your returns?

5. How important is loose change to you? Please explain.

6. How much money do you currently have in your pocket or purse? Is this important to know?

7. List everything you will need to buy during the next year. What is the estimated expenditure for each item?

8. How can you reduce expenditures from items on the list above?

9. Keep notes of all expenditures for at least one week.

10. Do you believe that money is "the root of all evil"? If you do, please explain.

Digging In

1. Prioritize both spending and saving based on your needs. Develop a spending budget so you do not deprive yourself.

2. Create a budget to allow for emergencies like severe illness or car repairs.

3. Start savings accounts for children at home and those at school. Invite a bank representative to your classroom to discuss the importance of saving and spending. Most banks will facilitate the accounts process in your school location.

4. Create a vacation account and make a deposit each pay period. As your balance grows, the more excited you will get about planning a well-deserved vacation.

5. Help students identify something they want to purchase—a gift for themselves or a family member—and help them work out a realistic savings plan to accomplish the goal.

16

Live Life with Urgency

LIVING LIFE WITH A SENSE OF URGENCY DOES NOT MEAN being fearful, stressed, anxious, or depressed. It means living your passion each day. The first step is to clarify your purpose, to understand who you are and what makes your heart smile.

In chapter 6, I shared a story of getting extremely ill, an experience that jolted me into making wiser decisions about foods and eating, exercising, thinking more positively, acknowledging and reducing stressful situations, and analyzing my relationships. Reflection also showed me that I was too comfortable. Yes, I was living my purpose, but I needed more. Therefore, I accepted a job as principal of an extremely low-performing school. I defied the critics who worked hard to discourage me. That was one of the best professional decisions I made. I was able to help children see beyond their circumstances and embrace learning. The action research from that school's transformation contributed to the debate about education in urban schools. Getting out of my comfort zone opened doors I only dreamed about.

Comparing yourself to others is draining. Focusing on other people's success takes time away from you being your champion. Emulate the good in others; create your own path. When I was a little girl, I wanted to be like my teachers because of what they represented. As I grew older, I learned to create my path using their examples. I never focused on what others could do for me but took charge of my values, goals, and aspirations.

When my family migrated to the United States of America and felt the throes of poverty, the easy thing to do was to cling to the safety of getting a weekly paycheck. Instead, I took a leap of faith and became a full-time college student to pursue a degree in education. My burning desire to follow my dreams overpowered my fears. Michael Jordan and Nike coined the trademark "Just Do It," and that's what we did.

I welcome the challenge of a new job. I was often the first to volunteer to teach another grade level or subject. In Jamaica, there is no middle school concept. Children leave elementary school and go to high school. I went to high school at eleven years old. As a result, my first experiences with middle school were through my children. Since my goal was to be an effective administrator, I requested a transfer to a middle school, knowing that I would be on a huge learning curve. My vulnerability pushed me to learn and grow.

I never knew the first step to writing a book. I believed that by sharing tips that influenced my life and career, I could help others. My first book, *7 Insider Secrets: Transform Your Low-Performing Elementary School and Score an "A" in Record Time* (Cover 2013), details processes and procedures of a school reform model that transformed a school. My goal with this book is to help teachers and other educators see that by working on personal behaviors, one can strengthen her career endeavors. I cannot wait to share my memoirs with the world. Writing is not easy, but success requires a force of will.

I once had an associate tell me that I was changing; I was no longer the person she first met. Initially, I was hurt and lost a few nights of sleep. Then I came to my senses. As we get older, we become wiser, with expanded experiences and new relationships. I thought I should change. My friend saw this as negative, and I finally realized that there was nothing wrong with me. Living a life of urgency involves purging that which is not working, embracing and adding new ideas and situations.

As mentioned, I love to travel; however, going to a country where people speak a different language and eat unfamiliar foods can be intimidating. Still, living a life of urgency provides the freedom to change your mind-set and live in the moment, to laugh at your mistakes and ignorance.

Social media can be distracting. It is easy to spend hours getting lost looking at pictures and reading ghastly stories of people you don't know. We get fascinated with people's Facebook pages or spend precious time seeing how many "likes" we received from a recent post. In the end, is getting lost on social media getting you closer to a goal? The message is not to waste time on things that do not matter.

In the introduction to college course I teach, one of the goals is to help students decide on or confirm a major of study. Class assignments include personal and career inventories, interviews with in-field experts, and identifying the ideal life with specific action steps. The assignments help students clarify their purpose.

Along with other adults, I once chaperoned a group of fifth-grade students to the Everglades in Florida. One activity was rowing down the Peace River. Well, I had never been in a canoe, and the sight of the murky water was terrifying. I was the teacher and had three students in my water vessel. The only option was to seize the moment. I had no time to ponder mistakes or think about looking silly. Later I used the experience as a teachable moment not to put things off.

I was clear at the age of five that I wanted to be a teacher, and I never strayed away from that dream. Many young children almost weekly change what they want to be when they grow up.

I advocate for exposing children to a vast number of careers that can be accomplished in activities like career days, guest speakers, field trips, research, and interviews. As a grade school teacher, I created a yearly extracurricular activity calendar aligned to curriculum objectives. I could then assign a classroom volunteer to make preliminary arrangements. Extension activities added real-world experiences to students' learning.

One of my favorite sayings, "I never got here by myself," is a reminder not to forget the people who sacrificed so that I would achieve more than they did. Each time I achieve a goal or get an award, I think about and express gratitude to my mother and father, who barely got to see the fruits of their labor. My only brother passed suddenly. It is important to cherish family and relationships. Shower your loved ones with appreciation and love take advantage of opportunities; there are many.

We all have something to contribute to this thing called life, but time is not limitless. Live with a sense of urgency, which will foster a healthier, more fulfilled, and happier journey. Teachers, your bags are heavy, but you do not have to carry them alone.

Teachers' Corner

1. If this were your last day on earth, how would you spend it?

2. What are your urgent needs?

3. If money were no object, what would you be doing?

4. If you had no obstacles, which are the most important problems you would commit to handling?

5. Is love an action? Please comment.

6. List factors that are preventing you from living your purpose.

7. Describe a time when you did not listen to your heart.

8. Is being selfish a bad thing? Why or why not?

9. How are you same or different from your younger self?

10. How do you instill in children that failure is part of life?

Digging In

1. Use the faculty room bulletin board as a public space on which people will use Post-it notes to make comments on specific topics. For example, "All children ...," Teachers are ...," "Before I leave this school, I want to ..."

2. Create a life purpose statement.

3. Which laws governing education would you change? Why?

4. Make a list of ten things for which you are grateful.

5. Talk with an expert about factors keeping you from living your best life.

Reference List

Alcott, Louisa May. 1880. *Little Women*. Brooklyn, New York: Boston: Roberts Brothers

Cover, Janice. 2013. *7 Insider Secrets: Transform Your Low-Performing Elementary School and Score an "A" in Record Time*. USA: Minna Press.

Carroll, Lewis. 1865. *Alice's Adventures in Wonderland*. New York: Macmillan Publishers

Dickens, Charles. 1996. *Great Expectations*. England: Clay Ltd.

Dixon, Franklin W. 2016. *Hardy Boys Adventure Series*. New York: Aladdin.

Harris, Kevin S. 2002. *Jamaican Words & Proverbs*. Kingston: LMH Publishing.

"He that spareth his rod hateth his son, but he that loveth him chasteneth him in good season." Proverbs 13:24, 21st Century King James Version.

Keene, Carolyn. 1930. *The Nancy Drew Mystery Stories*. New York: Aladdin.

Kuter, David J. February 2019. *Thrombotic Thrombocytopenia Purpura* (TTP). Retrieved from https://www.merckmanuals.com/professional/hematology-and-oncology/thrombocytopenia-and-platelet-dysfunction/thrombotic-thrombocytopenic-purpura-ttp.

Piper, Watty. 1976. *The Little Engine That Could*. New York: Platt & Munk.

Shakespeare, William. 1991. *The Merchant of Venice*. Leicester: Charnwood.

CPSIA information can be obtained
at www.ICGtesting.com
Printed in the USA
FSHW010407260320
68485FS